BENCHMARK SERIES

Microsoft® Excel®

2016
Level 2

Workbook

Davidson

PARADIGM
EDUCATION SOLUTIONS

St. Paul

Senior Vice President	Linda Hein
Editor in Chief	Christine Hurney
Director of Production	Timothy W. Larson
Production Editor	Jen Weaverling
Cover and Text Designer	Valerie King
Copy Editors	Communicáto, Ltd.
Senior Design and Production Specialist	Jack Ross
Design and Production Specialist	PerfecType
Assistant Developmental Editors	Mamie Clark, Katie Werdick
Testers	Janet Blum, Fanshawe College; Traci Post
Instructional Support Writers	Janet Blum, Fanshawe College; Brienna McWade
Indexer	Terry Casey
Vice President Information Technology	Chuck Bratton
Digital Projects Manager	Tom Modl
Vice President Sales and Marketing	Scott Burns
Director of Marketing	Lara Weber McLellan

ISBN 978-0-76386-940-3 (digital)
ISBN 978-0-76387-170-3 (print)

© 2017 by Paradigm Publishing, Inc.
875 Montreal Way
St. Paul, MN 55102
Email: educate@emcp.com
Website: ParadigmCollege.com

Contents

Microsoft® Excel® Level 2

Unit 1

Advanced Formatting, Formulas, and Data Management

Advanced Formatting Techniques

Study Tools

Study tools include a presentation and a list of chapter Quick Steps and Hint margin notes. Use these resources to help you further develop and review skills learned in this chapter.

Concepts Check

Check your understanding by identifying application tools used in this chapter. If you are a SNAP user, launch the Concepts Check from your Assignments page.

Recheck

Check your understanding by taking this quiz. If you are a SNAP user, launch the Recheck from your Assignments page.

Skills Exercise

Additional activities are available to SNAP users. If you are a SNAP user, access these activities from your Assignments page.

Skills Assessment

Assessment

1

Data Files

Use Conditional and Fraction Formatting

1. Open **RSRServRpt.xlsx**.
2. Save the workbook with the name **1-RSRServRpt**.
3. Apply the following formatting changes to the Sep worksheet:
   a. Format the values in the range C6:C23 as fractions using the As quarters (2/4) type.
   b. Format the rate codes in the range D6:D22 with the 3 Traffic Lights (Rimmed) icon set (second column, first row in the *Shapes* section.)
   c. Use the *New Rules* option to format the parts values in the range F6:F22 with the light red fill color (sixth column, second row) for those cells with values that are equal to 0.
   d. Format the total invoice values in the range G6:G22 using the red data bars. (Use the *Red Data Bar* option in the *Gradient Fill* section of the Data Bars side menu.)
4. Save, print, and then close **1-RSRServRpt.xlsx**.

Apply Custom Number Formatting

1. Open **1-RSRServRpt.xlsx**.
2. Save the workbook with the name **1-RSRServRpt-2**.
3. Create and apply the following custom number formats to the Sep worksheet:
   a. Create a custom number format that displays *hrs* one space after each value in the range C6:C23. ***Hint: After selecting*** Custom ***in the*** Category ***list box, click after the existing format codes in the*** Type ***text box and then add the required entry. (Do not delete what is already in the*** Type ***text box.)***
   b. Create a custom number format that displays *RSR-* in front of each work order number in the range B6:B22.
4. Save, print, and then close **1-RSRServRpt-2.xlsx**.

Use Custom AutoFilter and Filter and Sort by Color

1. Open **1-RSRServRpt-2.xlsx**.
2. Save the workbook with the name **1-RSRServRpt-3**.
3. Make the following changes to the Sep worksheet:
   a. Select the range A5:G22 and turn on the Filter feature.
   b. Using the filter arrow at the top of the *Hours Billed* column, display those invoices for which the hours billed are between 1.75 and 3.75. ***Hint: When typing in the values, type*** 1.75 ***and*** 3.75. ***Do not select*** 1 3/4 **hrs** ***and*** 3 3/4 **hrs** *from the drop-down lists in the Custom AutoFilter dialog box.*
4. Make the following changes to the Oct worksheet:
   a. Select the range A5:G22 and then turn on the Filter feature.
   b. Filter the *Parts* column by color to show only those invoices for which no parts were billed.
5. Make the following changes to the Nov worksheet:
   a. Clear the filter from the *Date* column.
   b. Filter the worksheet by the icon associated with rate code 3.
6. Make the following changes to the Dec worksheet:
   a. Remove the filter arrows from the worksheet.
   b. Make any cell within the range A5:G22 active.
   c. Open the Sort dialog box.
   d. Define three sort levels as follows:

Sort by	*Sort On*	*Order*
rate code	cell icon	red traffic light on top
rate code	cell icon	yellow traffic light on top
rate code	cell icon	green traffic light on top

7. Print the workbook.
8. Save and then close **1-RSRServRpt-3.xlsx**.

Create, Edit, and Delete Formatting Rules

1. Open **VRPay-Oct27.xlsx**.
2. Save the workbook with the name **1-VRPay-Oct27**.
3. Create and apply two conditional formatting rules for the values in the *Pay Rate* column as follows:
   a. Apply a light blue fill color (fifth column, third row) to values between 10.50 and 12.00.
   b. Apply a light green fill color (seventh column, third row) to values greater than 12.00.

4. Create a conditional formatting rule for the *Gross Pay* column that will format the values in the dark red font color (first option in the *Standard Colors* section) for those employees that have worked overtime hours. ***Hint: When entering the formula use relative referencing (K6:K23) in the logical test.***

5. Use the Quick Analysis button to find the top 10% among values in the *Gross Pay* column.

6. Edit the formatting rule for *Cell Value <10.5* in the *Pay Rate* column by applying the light orange fill color (tenth column, third row).

7. Use the Quick Analysis button to delete the formatting rule for *Overtime Hours* column.

8. Save, print, and then close **1-VRPay-Oct27.xlsx**.

Use Text Functions to Extract and Combine Data

Assessment

5

Data Files

1. Open **RSREmail.xlsx**.
2. Save the workbook with the name **1-RSREmail**.
3. Extract data to begin the process of creating new email addresses as follows:
   a. In column D, use the LEFT function to extract the first letter of the first name found in column A.
   b. In column E, use the LEFT function to extract the first four letters of the last name found in column B.
   c. In column F, use the RIGHT function to extract the last two numbers of the cell phone number found in column C.
4. In column G, use the CONCATENATE function to combine the text, numbers, and additional characters in the following order:
   a. The first letter of the first name found in column D.
   b. A period.
   c. The first four letters of the last name found in column E.
   d. The last two numbers of the cell phone number found in column F.
   e. The @ symbol and domain name ParadigmCollege.net.
5. Use the fill handle to copy the formulas in the range D6:G6 into the range D7:G29.
6. Save, print, and then close **1-RSREmail.xlsx**.

Visual Benchmark

Data Files

Format a Billing Summary

1. Open **BillingsOct1to5.xlsx**.
2. Save the workbook with the name **1-BillingsOct1to5**.
3. Format the worksheet to match the one shown in Figure WB-1.1 using the following information:
   - The data in the *Billing Code* column has been custom formatted to add the text *Amicus#-* in the standard blue font color in front of the code number.
   - Icon sets have been used in the *Attorney Code* column and the same icon set should be applied in the *Attorney Code Table* section of the worksheet.
   - The data bars added to the values in the *Legal Fees* column have been formatted with the Turquoise, Accent 3 gradient fill (seventh column, first row in the *Theme Colors* section). ***Hint: Select More Rules in the Data Bars side menu.***
   - Values below 1500.00 in the *Total Due* column have been conditionally formatted and the worksheet has been sorted by the font color used for the conditional format.
4. Save, print, and then close **1-BillingsOct1to5**.

Figure WB-1.1 Visual Benchmark

	B	C	D	E	F	G	H	I	J
1				O'DONOVAN & SULLIVAN LAW ASSOCIATES					
2				BILLING SUMMARY					
3				OCTOBER 1 TO 5, 2018					
4	Client	Date	Billing Code	Attorney Code	Legal Fees	Disbursements	Total Due		Billing Code Table
5	10106	10/1/2018	Amicus#-3	1	1,028.50	23.75	1,052.25	Code	Area of Practice
6	10225	10/2/2018	Amicus#-5	3	1,211.00	37.85	1,248.85	1	Corporate
7	10341	10/3/2018	Amicus#-1	2	1,143.75	55.24	1,198.99	2	Divorce & Separation
8	10210	10/4/2018	Amicus#-6	3	1,450.00	24.25	1,474.25	3	Wills & Estates
9	10125	10/5/2018	Amicus#-1	2	1,143.75	38.12	1,181.87	4	Real Estate
10	10346	10/5/2018	Amicus#-6	3	1,425.00	62.18	1,487.18	5	Employment Litigation
11	10384	10/5/2018	Amicus#-4	4	1,237.50	34.28	1,271.78	6	Insurance Personal Injury
12	10104	10/1/2018	Amicus#-2	1	2,273.75	95.10	2,368.85	7	Other
13	10125	10/1/2018	Amicus#-1	2	2,493.75	55.40	2,549.15		
14	10210	10/2/2018	Amicus#-6	3	2,425.00	65.20	2,490.20		Attorney Code Table
15	10285	10/2/2018	Amicus#-4	4	3,807.00	48.96	3,855.96	Code	Attorney
16	10334	10/3/2018	Amicus#-1	2	1,518.75	27.85	1,546.60	1	Marty O'Donovan
17	10420	10/3/2018	Amicus#-7	3	2,500.00	34.95	2,534.95	2	Toni Sullivan
18	10425	10/3/2018	Amicus#-4	4	2,043.00	38.75	2,081.75	3	Rosa Martinez
19	10225	10/4/2018	Amicus#-5	3	2,300.00	42.15	2,342.15	4	Kyle Williams
20	10290	10/4/2018	Amicus#-7	3	1,620.00	65.15	1,685.15		
21	10278	10/4/2018	Amicus#-2	1	2,040.00	85.47	2,125.47		
22	10358	10/5/2018	Amicus#-1	2	1,762.50	55.24	1,817.74		
23	10495	10/5/2018	Amicus#-3	3	2,375.00	94.55	2,469.55		

Case Study

Part 1

Data Files

Yolanda Robertson, your manager at NuTrends Market Research, has provided a workbook named **USIncomeStats.xlsx**. It contains data Yolanda obtained from the US Census Bureau with the two-year average median household income by state for 2013. Open the workbook and save it with the name **1-USIncomeStats-CS**. Yolanda wants you to format the data using colors to differentiate income levels. She has proposed the following categories, to which you should apply color formatting of your choosing:

> *Average Median Income Range*
>
> Less than $45,000
>
> Between $45,000 and $55,000
>
> Greater than $55,000

Apply color formatting using conditional formatting, since Yolanda may change these salary ranges after she reviews the data and you want to be able to edit the formatting rule if that happens. Choose colors that will be easy to distinguish from one another. Create a reference table starting in cell E3 that provides Yolanda with a legend that identifies the colors used. For example, in cell E3 type Less than 45,000, in cell H3 type a sample value (such as 35,000), and then format each cell using the color that represents the formatting you applied to the rule category. Save and then print the worksheet. *Note: If you submit your work in hard copy and do not have access to a color printer, write on the printout the color format you applied to each category.*

Part 2

Yolanda has reviewed the worksheet from Part 1 and has asked you to do some further work. Before you change the file, you make a copy of it in case that data can be used for another purpose. Save the workbook with the name **1-USIncomeStats-CS2**. Use this workbook to make the modifications. Yolanda wants you to sort the worksheet by color, with the color representing the *Greater than $55,000* group on top, followed by the *Between $45,000 and $55,000* group and then the *Less than $45,000* group. Do not include the entries in row 3 for the US average in the sorted list. After sorting the worksheet, filter the median incomes to display the top 20 states. **Hint: Customize the value in the Top 10 AutoFilter**. Yolanda also wants you to add a contact telephone list next to the top 20 state data. Create the list below using the following telephone numbers and a special number format. Place them in a suitable location. Adjust the column width so the numbers can be seen.

Yolanda (cell)	800 555 3117
Yolanda (office)	800 555 4629
Yolanda (home)	800 555 2169
Yolanda (fax)	800 555 6744

Part 3

Continuing with the worksheet formatted in Part 2 of this Case Study, you decide to experiment with the filtered census data worksheet to see if formatting using color scales will highlight the spread between the highest and lowest median incomes more distinctly. Apply conditional formatting using a two- or three-color scale to the filtered cells in column C. (Exclude the US median income at the top of the column.) Remove the outdated legend and clear any formatting. Save the workbook with the name **1-USIncomeStats-CS3**. Print the worksheet. *Note: If you submit your work in hard copy and do not have access to a color printer, write on the printout the two- or three-color scale conditional formatting you applied to the filtered values in column C.*

Part 4

Yolanda is preparing a training seminar for new market researchers hired at NuTrends Market Research. So she can provide background material for the training on US Census Bureau statistics, Yolanda has asked you to research the history of the bureau. Using the Internet, go to www.census.gov/ and find the page that describes the history of the US Census Bureau. *Hint: Explore the tabbed pages at the* <u>History</u> *hyperlink under ABOUT US at the bottom of the home page*. In a new sheet in the same file as the median income data, type in column A five to seven interesting facts about the bureau from the website. Adjust the width of column A and apply the formatting option *Wrap Text* or *Shrink Text to Fit* to improve the appearance of the worksheet. In column C, use a text function to convert the text to upper case. Apply the same formatting options used in column A to improve the appearance of the worksheet. Save the revised workbook and name it **1-USIncomeStats-CS4**. Print the worksheet and then close the workbook.

Study Tools

Study tools include a presentation and a list of chapter Quick Steps and Hint margin notes. Use these resources to help you further develop and review skills learned in this chapter.

Concepts Check

Check your understanding by identifying application tools used in this chapter. If you are a SNAP user, launch the Concepts Check from your Assignments page.

Recheck

Check your understanding by taking this quiz. If you are a SNAP user, launch the Recheck from your Assignments page.

Skills Exercise

Additional activities are available to SNAP users. If you are a SNAP user, access these activities from your Assignments page.

Skills Assessment

Assessment

1

Data Files

Create Range Names and Use the Lookup Function

Note: If you submit your work as hard copy, check with your instructor before printing assessments to see if you need to print two copies: one with numbers displayed and another with cell formulas displayed.

1. Open **RSROctLabor.xlsx**.
2. Save the workbook with the name **2-RSROctLabor**.
3. Modify the range named *LaborCost* to include cell F22.
4. Change the range name for the range named *Hr* to *Hours*.
5. In cell E7, create a VLOOKUP formula to return the correct hourly rate based on the technician code in cell D7. Use the range name *RateChart* within the formula to reference the hourly rate chart. Make sure Excel will return values for exact matches only.
6. Create or copy the following formulas:
   a. Copy the VLOOKUP formula in cell E7 and paste it into the range E8:E22.
   b. In cell F7, multiply the values in the range named *Hours* by the hourly rate in cell E7. Add the ROUND function to ensure that all labor costs are rounded to the nearest cent (two decimal places).
   c. Copy the formula in cell F7 and paste it into the range F8:F22.
   d. Create the formula in cell F23 to sum the values in the column.
7. Preview and then print the worksheet.
8. Save and then close **2-RSROctLabor.xlsx**.

Use Conditional Statistical and Math Functions

Note: For all the functions in Assessment 2 except those in Step 3, use range names in the formulas to reference sources.

1. Open **2-RSROctLabor.xlsx**.
2. Save the workbook with the name **2-RSROctLabor-2**.
3. Using the range named *TechCode*, create COUNTIF formulas in these cells:
   - I9: Count the number of calls made by technician 1.
   - I10: Count the number of calls made by technician 2.
   - I11: Count the number of calls made by technician 3.
4. In cell I14, create a COUNTIFS formula to count the number of calls made by technician 3 for which the hours logged were greater than three. Use range names (*TechCode* and *Hours*) where possible.
5. Using the ranges named *TechCode* and *LaborCost*, create SUMIF formulas in these cells:
   - J9: Add the labor cost for calls made by technician 1.
   - J10: Add the labor cost for calls made by technician 2.
   - J11: Add the labor cost for calls made by technician 3.
6. Using the ranges named *TechCode*, *LaborCost*, and *Hours*, create a SUMIFS formula in cell J14 to add the labor cost for calls made by technician 3 (criteria 1) in which the hours logged were greater than three (criteria 2).
7. Using the named ranges *TechCode* and *LaborCost*, create AVERAGEIF formulas in these cells:
   - J18: Average the labor cost for calls made by technician 1.
   - J19: Average the labor cost for calls made by technician 2.
   - J20: Average the labor cost for calls made by technician 3.
8. Ensure that the Comma format has been applied to the cells or ranges:
   - J9:J11
   - J14
   - J18:J20
9. Save, print, and then close **2-RSROctLabor-2.xlsx**.

Use the PMT and PPMT Financial Functions

1. Open **PrecisionWarehouse.xlsx**.
2. Save the workbook with the name **2-PrecisionWarehouse.xlsx**.
3. Using cell references, create a PMT formula in cell D8 to calculate the monthly loan payment for a proposed loan from NewVentures Capital Inc. *Note: The PMT function uses the same arguments as the PPMT function with the exception that there is no **Per** criterion. Remember to divide the rate by 12 and multiply the nper by 12 to use monthly units.*
4. Using cell references, create PPMT formulas to find the principal portion of the loan payment for the first loan payment in cell D10 and the last loan payment in cell D11.
5. In cell D13, create a formula to calculate the total cost of the loan by multiplying the monthly loan payment times the amortization period in years times 12.
6. Print the worksheet.
7. Save and then close **2-PrecisionWarehouse.xlsx**.

Use Logical Functions

1. Open **ACPremiumReview.xlsx**.
2. Save the workbook with the name **2-ACPremiumReview.xlsx**. The following range names have been created:

B4:B23	*Claims*
C4:C23	*AtFault*
D4:D23	*Rating*
E4:E23	*Deductible*

3. Using named ranges, create a formula in cell G4 to display *Yes* if the number of at-fault claims is greater than one and the current rating is greater than two. Both conditions must test true to display *Yes*; otherwise, display *No* in the cell. ***Hint: Use a nested IF and AND formula***.
4. Using named ranges, create a formula in cell H4 to display *Yes* in the cell if either the number of claims is greater than two or the current deductible is less than $1,000.00; otherwise, display *No* in the cell. ***Hint: Use a nested IF and OR formula***.
5. Center the results in cells G4 and H4 and then copy and paste the formulas into the ranges G5:G23 and H5:H23, respectively. Deselect the range after copying.
6. Save, print, and then close **2-ACPremiumReview.xlsx**.

Use the HLOOKUP Function

1. Open **JTutorProgressRpt.xlsx**.
2. Save the workbook with the name **2-JTutorProgressRpt**.
3. Make ProgressComments the active worksheet and review the layout of the lookup table. Notice that the data is organized in rows, with the scores in row 1 and the grade comments in row 2.
4. Select the range A1:G2 and type GradeTable as the range name.
5. Deselect the range and then make StudentProgress the active worksheet.
6. Create a formula in cell G4 that looks up the student's total score in the range named *GradeTable* and returns the appropriate progress comment.
7. Copy the formula in cell G4 and paste it into the range G5:G12. Deselect the range.
8. Save, print, and then close **2-JTutorProgressRpt.xlsx**.

Visual Benchmark

Use Lookup, Statistical, and Math Functions in a Billing Summary

1. Open **BillHrsOct1to5.xlsx**.
2. Save the workbook with the name **2-BillHrsOct1to5**.
3. Review the worksheet shown in Figure WB-2.1. Use the following information to create the required formulas. Create range names to use in all the formulas so readers can easily interpret the formula:

    - In column F, create a formula to look up the attorney's hourly rate from the table at the bottom right of the worksheet. The formula should return results for exact matches only.

    - In column G, calculate the legal fees billed by multiplying the billable hours times the hourly rate.

    - In the range J6:J9, calculate the total legal fees billed by attorney.

    - In the range J13:J16, calculate the average hours billed by attorney.

4. Save, print, and then close **2-BillHrsOct1to5.xlsx**.

Figure WB-2.1 Visual Benchmark 1

	A	B	C	D	E	F	G	H	I	J
1					O'DONOVAN & SULLIVAN LAW ASSOCIATES					
2					BILLING SUMMARY					
3					OCTOBER 1 TO 5, 2018					
4	File	Client	Date	Attorney Code	Billable Hours	Hourly Rate	Legal Fees	Billing Statistics		
5	FL-325	10104	10/1/2018	1	26.75	185.00	4,948.75	Total Legal Fees Billed by Attorney		
6	EP-652	10106	10/1/2018	1	12.10	185.00	2,238.50	1	Marty O'Donovan	$ 11,627.25
7	CL-412	10125	10/1/2018	2	33.25	175.00	5,818.75	2	Toni Sullivan	$ 18,812.50
8	IN-745	10210	10/2/2018	3	24.25	210.00	5,092.50	3	Rosa Martinez	$ 32,142.60
9	EL-632	10225	10/2/2018	3	12.11	210.00	2,543.10	4	Kyle Williams	$ 14,962.50
10	RE-475	10285	10/2/2018	4	42.30	190.00	8,037.00		TOTAL	$ 77,544.85
11	CL-501	10341	10/3/2018	2	15.25	175.00	2,668.75			
12	CL-521	10334	10/3/2018	2	20.25	175.00	3,543.75	Average Billable Hours by Attorney		
13	PL-348	10420	10/3/2018	3	25.00	210.00	5,250.00	1	Marty O'Donovan	20.95
14	RE-492	10425	10/3/2018	4	22.70	190.00	4,313.00	2	Toni Sullivan	21.50
15	EL-632	10225	10/4/2018	3	23.00	210.00	4,830.00	3	Rosa Martinez	19.13
16	PL-512	10290	10/4/2018	3	16.20	210.00	3,402.00	4	Kyle Williams	26.25
17	IN-745	10210	10/4/2018	3	14.50	210.00	3,045.00			
18	FL-385	10278	10/4/2018	1	24.00	185.00	4,440.00	Attorney Code Table		
19	CL-412	10125	10/5/2018	2	15.25	175.00	2,668.75	Code	Attorney	Hourly Rate
20	CL-450	10358	10/5/2018	2	23.50	175.00	4,112.50	1	Marty O'Donovan	185.00
21	IN-801	10346	10/5/2018	3	14.25	210.00	2,992.50	2	Toni Sullivan	175.00
22	EP-685	10495	10/5/2018	3	23.75	210.00	4,987.50	3	Rosa Martinez	210.00
23	RE-501	10384	10/5/2018	4	13.75	190.00	2,612.50	4	Kyle Williams	190.00
24				TOTAL	402.16	TOTAL $	77,544.85			

Activity 2

Data Files

Use Lookup and Logical Functions to Calculate Cardiology Costs

1. Open **WPMCCardioCosts.xlsx**.
2. Save the workbook with the name **2-WPMCCardioCosts**.
3. Range names for this worksheet have already been created. Spend a few moments reviewing the range names and the cells each name references to become familiar with the worksheet.
4. Review the worksheet shown in Figure WB-2.2 and revise it to match the one shown by creating formulas using the following information:

   - In column G, create a formula to look up the surgery fee in the table at the bottom of the worksheet. The formula should return results for exact matches only.

   - In column H, insert the cost of the aortic or mitral valve if the cardiac surgery required a replacement valve; otherwise, place a 0 in the cell. *Hint: The surgery codes for surgeries that include replacement valves are ART and MRT (for aortic and mitral, respectively).*

   - In column I, calculate the postoperative hospital cost by multiplying the number of days the patient was in hospital by the postoperative cost per day.

   - In column J, calculate the total cost as the sum of the surgery fee, valve cost, and postoperative hospital cost.

   - Calculate the total cost for each column in row 22.

5. Format the numbers as shown in Figure WB-2.2.
6. Save, print, and then close **2-WPMCCardioCosts.xlsx**.

Figure WB-2.2 Visual Benchmark 2

	A	B	C	D	E	F	G	H	I	J
1					Wellington Park Medical Center					
2					Division of Cardiology					
3					Adult Cardiac Surgery Costs					
4	Month:	October	Surgeon:	Novak						
5	Patient Number	Patient Last Name	Patient First Name	Surgery Code	Days in Hospital		Surgery Fee	Valve Cost	Postoperative Hospital Cost	Total Cost
6	60334124	Wagner	Sara	MRP	7		$ 5,325.00	$ -	$ 6,996.50	$ 12,321.50
7	60334567	Gonzalez	Hector	ARP	10		4,876.00	-	9,995.00	14,871.00
8	60398754	Vezina	Paula	ABP	5		4,820.00	-	4,997.50	9,817.50
9	60347821	Dowling	Jager	MRT	11		6,240.00	875.00	10,994.50	18,109.50
10	60328192	Ashman	Carl	ARP	4		4,876.00	-	3,998.00	8,874.00
11	60321349	Kaiser	Lana	ART	12		6,190.00	875.00	11,994.00	19,059.00
12	60398545	Van Bomm	Emile	ABP	7		4,820.00	-	6,996.50	11,816.50
13	60342548	Youngblood	Frank	ABP	6		4,820.00	-	5,997.00	10,817.00
14	60331569	Lorimar	Hannah	MRT	8		6,240.00	875.00	7,996.00	15,111.00
15	60247859	Peterson	Mark	ART	9		6,190.00	875.00	8,995.50	16,060.50
16	60158642	O'Connor	Terry	ABP	7		4,820.00	-	6,996.50	11,816.50
17	60458962	Jenkins	Esther	MRP	9		5,325.00	-	8,995.50	14,320.50
18	68521245	Norfolk	Leslie	ABP	8		4,820.00	-	7,996.00	12,816.00
19	63552158	Adams-Wiley	Susan	MRT	6		6,240.00	875.00	5,997.00	13,112.00
20	68451278	Estevez	Stefan	ARP	6		4,876.00	-	5,997.00	10,873.00
21										
22		Postoperative hospital cost per day:		$ 999.50		Total Cost:	$ 80,478.00	$4,375.00	$ 114,942.50	$199,795.50
23		Aortic or mitral valve cost:		$ 875.00						
24										
25		Surgery Code	Surgery Fee	Surgery Procedure						
26		ABP	4,820	Artery Bypass						
27		ARP	4,876	Aortic Valve Repair						
28		ART	6,190	Aortic Valve Replacement						
29		MRP	5,325	Mitral Valve Repair						
30		MRT	6,240	Mitral Valve Replacement						

Case Study

Part

1

Data Files

Yolanda Robertson, your manager at NuTrends Market Research, has been pleased with your previous work and has assigned you to a project with a new client. Yolanda is preparing a marketing plan for a franchise expansion for the owners of Pizza By Mario. The franchise was started in Michigan and has stores in Ohio, Wisconsin, and Iowa. The owners plan to double the number of locations within the next two years by expanding into neighboring states. The owners have provided a confidential franchise sales report to Yolanda in an Excel file named **PBMSales.xlsx**. Yolanda needs your help with Excel to extract some statistics and calculate franchise royalty payments. With this information, Yolanda will develop a franchise communication package for prospective franchisees.

Open the workbook and save it with the name **2-PBMSales**. Yolanda has asked for the following statistics and wants you to read the instructions found on the next page before you begin.

- A count of the number of stores with sales greater than $500,000
- A count of the number of stores located in Michigan with sales greater than $500,000
- Average sales for the stores in Detroit, Michigan
- Average sales for the Michigan stores established prior to 2004
- Total sales for the stores established prior to 2012
- Total sales for the Michigan stores established prior to 2012

Create the formulas on the previous page for Yolanda in rows 3 to 16 of columns H and I. Create range names for the data so Yolanda will be able to easily understand the formula when she reviews the worksheet. You determine the layout, labels, and other formats for the statistics section. The royalty rate and fee will be completed in Part 2. Save and print the worksheet.

Part 2

In the marketing package for new prospects, Yolanda plans to include sample sales figures and related franchise royalty payments. Pizza By Mario charges each store a royalty percentage based on its annual sales. As sales increase, the royalty percentage increases. For example, a store that sells $430,000 pays a royalty of 2% of sales, while a store that sells $765,000 pays a royalty of 5% of sales. A royalty rate table is included in the worksheet. Create a range name for the table and then create a lookup formula to insert the correct royalty percentage for each store in column F. Next, create a formula to calculate the dollar amount of the royalty payment based on the store's sales multiplied by the percentage in column F. Format the royalty percentage and royalty fee columns appropriately. Save the revised workbook with the name **2-PBMSales2**. Print the worksheet.

Part 3

Use the Help feature to learn about the MEDIAN and STDEV functions. Yolanda would like to calculate further statistics in a separate worksheet. Copy the range A2:E29 to Sheet2, keeping the source column widths. Using the sales data in column E, calculate the following statistics: (You determine the layout, labels, and other formats.)

- Average sales
- Maximum store sales
- Minimum store sales
- Median store sales
- Standard deviation of the sales data

Create one text box below the statistics and write an explanation in the box to explain what the median and standard deviation numbers mean based on what you learned by researching in Help. Print the worksheet, making sure that all the data fits on one page. Save the revised workbook with the name **2-PBMSales3**.

Part 4

Choose two states near Michigan, Ohio, Wisconsin, and/or Iowa and find statistics on the Internet that Yolanda can use to prepare a marketing plan for expanding Pizza By Mario into these states. For two cities in each new state, find population and income statistics. In a new worksheet within the Pizza By Mario franchise workbook, prepare a summary of your research findings. Using named ranges you create and an AVERAGEIF function, calculate the average of the mean household income for each state. Include in the worksheet the URLs of the sites from which you obtained your data, in case Yolanda wants to explore the links for further details. Print the worksheet, making sure that all the data fits on one page. Save the revised workbook with the name **2-PBMSales4**. Close the workbook.

Skills Assessment

Assessment

1

Data Files

Create and Format a Table

1. Open **VRSeries.xlsx**.
2. Save the workbook with the name **3-VRSeries**.
3. Select the range A4:K29 and create a table using the Format as Table button and the Table Style Medium 12 table style (fifth column, second row in the *Medium* section). The table has headers.
4. Add a calculated column to the table in column L by completing the following steps:
   a. Type Discount as the column heading in cell L4.
   b. Create a formula in the first record that multiplies the price in column J times the current discount in column K. The formula will copy to the rest of the rows in the table. Format the new values by applying the Comma format and specifying two digits after the decimal point.
   c. Type Sale Price as the column heading in cell M4.
   d. Create a formula in the first record that subtracts the discount in column L from the price in column J. The formula will copy to the rest of the rows in the table.
   e. Adjust the three title rows above the table to merge and center across columns A through M. Adjust all the column widths using AutoFit.
5. Add banding to the columns, remove banding from the rows, and emphasize the last column in the table.
6. Add a *Total* row to the table. Add an average function that calculates the average sale price. Delete the contents of cell A30 and type Average.

7. The DVD for *Grimm* cannot be located and the manager would like you to remove the record from the table. Delete the row in the table for the record with stock number CV-1019.

8. Save, print, and then close **3-VRSeries.xlsx**.

Assessment 2

Use Data Tools

1. Open **3-VRSeries.xlsx**.
2. Save the workbook with the name **3-VRSeries-2**.
3. Make the following changes:
   a. Insert a new blank column to the right of the column containing the combined season number and number of episodes and change the column headings to *Season No.* and *Episodes*, respectively.
   b. Split the *SeasonNo./Episodes* column into two columns (S# and E#).
4. Create the following validation rules:
   a. A custom format of "CV-"#### has been applied to the stock numbers. Create a validation rule for the *Stock No.* column that ensures all new entries are four characters in length. (With a custom number format, it is not necessary to include the characters between the quotation marks in the text length.)
   b. Add this input message to the column: Enter the last four digits of the stock number. Use the default error alert options.
   c. Create a drop-down list for the *Genre* column with the entries provided. Do not enter an input message, and use the default error alert options.
5. Add the record below to the table to test the data validation rules. (Initially enter incorrect values in the *Stock No.*, and *Genre* columns to make sure the rule and the messages work correctly.)

Stock No.	CV-1026
Title	Supernatural
Season No.	S11
Episodes	E23
Year Aired	2016-17
Genre	Horror
DVD	Yes
Blu-ray	Yes
Download	Yes
Multiformat	Yes
Price	34.99
Discount	(leave blank)

6. Use the Remove Duplicates feature to find and remove any duplicate rows using *Stock No.* as the comparison column.
7. Save, print, and then close **3-VRSeries-2.xlsx**.

Assessment 3

Subtotal Records

1. Open **3-VRSeries-2.xlsx**.
2. Save the workbook with the name **3-VRSeries-3**.
3. Remove the *Total* row and remove the emphasis from the last column in the table.
4. Convert the table to a normal range.
5. Adjust all column widths using AutoFit.
6. Sort the list first by the genre, then by the title, and then by the season number. Use the default sort values and sort order for each level.
7. Using the Subtotal button in the Outline group on the Data tab, add subtotals to the *Sale Price* column to calculate the average sale price and to count the number of TV shows by genre.

8. Display the worksheet at level 2 of the outline.
9. Show the details for the Comedy and Drama genres.
10. Print the worksheet.
11. Save and then close **3-VRSeries-3.xlsx**.

Visual Benchmark

Using Table and Data Tools in a Call List

1. Open **WPMCallList.xlsx**.
2. Save the workbook with the name **3-WPMCallList**.
3. Format and apply data tools as required to duplicate the worksheet in Figure WB-3.1 using the following information:
   - The worksheet has the *Table Style Medium 5* style applied to the table range.
   - Look closely at the sorted order. The table is sorted by three levels using the fields *Designation*, *Hourly Rate*, and *Hire Date*.
   - The shift cost equals the hourly rate times eight hours.
   - Use Flash Fill to split the names into two columns.
   - Include the *Total* row and apply the appropriate banded options.
4. Save, print, and then close **3-WPMCallList.xlsx**.

Figure WB-3.1 Visual Benchmark 1

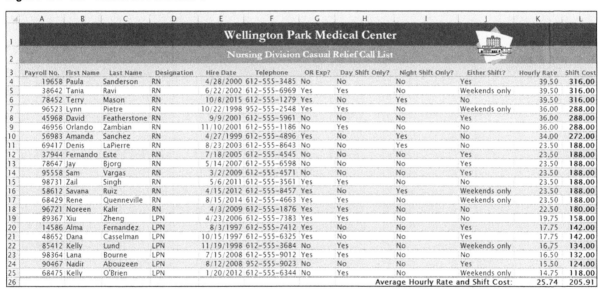

Using Subtotals in a Call List

1. Open **3-WPMCallList.xlsx**.
2. Save the workbook with the name **3-WPMCallList-2**.
3. Create subtotals and view the revised worksheet at the appropriate level to display as shown in Figure WB-3.2.
4. Save, print, and then close **3-WPMCallList-2.xlsx**.

Figure WB-3.2 Visual Benchmark 2

	A	B	C	D	E	F	G	H	I	J	K	L
1						Wellington Park Medical Center						
2						Nursing Division Casual Relief Call List						
3	Payroll No.	First Name	Last Name	Designation	Hire Date	Telephone	OR Exp?	Day Shift Only?	Night Shift Only?	Either Shift?	Hourly Rate	Shift Cost
19				RN Average							29.83	238.67
27				LPN Average							16.96	135.71
28				Grand Average							25.74	205.91

Case Study

Rajiv Patel, Vice-President of NuTrends Market Research, has sent you a file named **NuTrendsMktPlans.xlsx**. The workbook contains client information for the company's first-quarter marketing plans for three marketing consultants. Rajiv would like you to improve the reporting in the file by completing the following tasks:

- Set up the data as a table sorted first by the consultant's last name and then by the start date of the marketing campaign, both in ascending order. Rajiv would prefer that the consultant names be split into two columns.
- Improve the formatting of the dollar values.
- Add a *Total* row to sum the values in the columns that contain dollar amounts.
- Add formatting to the titles above the table that is well suited to the colors in the table style you selected.
- Make any other formatting changes you think will improve the appearance of the worksheet.

Save the revised workbook with the name **3-NuTrendsMktPlans**. Print the worksheet in landscape orientation with the width scaled to one page.

Rajiv would like statistics for each consultant added to **3-NuTrendsMktPlans.xlsx**. Specifically, he would like to see the following information:

- The total marketing plan budget values being managed by each consultant, as well as the total planned expenditures by month
- The average marketing plan budget being managed by each consultant, as well as the average planned expenditures by month

Rajiv would like a printout that displays only the total and average values for each consultant, as well as the grand average and grand total. Save the revised workbook with the name **3-NuTrendsMktPlans-2**. Print and then close the worksheet.

In addition, Rajiv has asked that you provide another report from the file named **NuTrendsMktPlans.xlsx**. Specifically, he would like a printout of the worksheet that shows the original data at the top of the worksheet and a few blank rows below the worksheet. Rajiv would like to see the marketing plan details for Yolanda Robertson's clients that have campaigns starting after January 31, 2018.

Research in Help how to filter a range of cells using the Advanced Filter button in the Sort & Filter group on the Data tab. Make sure you read how to copy rows that meet your filter criteria to another area of the worksheet. Using the information you have learned, open **NuTrendsMktPlans.xlsx**, insert three new rows above the worksheet, and use these rows to create the criteria range. Filter the list according to Rajiv's specifications. Rows that meet the criteria should be copied below the worksheet starting in cell A21. Add an appropriate title to describe the copied data in cell A20. Make any formatting changes you think will improve the appearance of the worksheet. Save the revised workbook with the name **3-NuTrendsMktPlans-3**. Print the worksheet and then close the workbook.

Part 4

Rajiv is looking for information on current salary ranges for market researchers in the United States. Use the Internet to find this information. If possible, find salary information that is specific to your state for a minimum of three cities or regions. Find a low salary and high salary for a market researcher in each city or region.

Create a workbook that summarizes the results of your research. Include the website addresses as hyperlinked cells next to the items about salary ranges. Organize the data in the workbook as a table. Apply table formatting so the data is attractively presented and easy to read. Add a *Total* row and include an Average function to find the average salary from the three cities. Find a minimum of three and a maximum of five resources. Save the workbook with the name **3-NuTrendsSalaryAnalysis**. Print the worksheet and then close the workbook.

Summarizing and Consolidating Data

Study Tools

Study tools include a presentation and a list of chapter Quick Steps and Hint margin notes. Use these resources to help you further develop and review skills learned in this chapter.

Concepts Check

Check your understanding by identifying application tools used in this chapter. If you are a SNAP user, launch the Concepts Check from your Assignments page.

Recheck

Check your understanding by taking this quiz. If you are a SNAP user, launch the Recheck from your Assignments page.

Skills Exercise

Additional activities are available to SNAP users. If you are a SNAP user, access these activities from your Assignments page.

Skills Assessment

Assessment

1

Data Files

Summarize Data in Multiple Worksheets Using Range Names

1. Open **NADQ1Fees.xlsx**.
2. Save the workbook with the name **4-NADQ1Fees-1**.
3. The workbook contains three worksheets showing dental fees earned in January, February, and March for three dentists at a dental clinic. Create a range name in cell E13 of each worksheet to reference the total fees earned by each dentist for the quarter as follows:
   a. Type PopovichTotal as the name for cell E13 in the Popovich worksheet.
   b. Type VanketTotal as the name for cell E13 in the Vanket worksheet.
   c. Type JovanovicTotal as the name for cell E13 in the Jovanovic worksheet.
4. Make FeeSummary the active worksheet and then type the following label in cell A6: Quarter 1 fees for Popovich, Vanket, and Jovanovic.
5. Make cell F6 the active cell and create a Sum formula to calculate the total fees earned by each dentist using the range names created in Step 3.
6. Apply the Accounting format to cell F6 and then autofit the width of the column.
7. Print the FeeSummary worksheet.
8. Save and then close **4-NADQ1Fees-1.xlsx**.

Assessment 2

Summarize Data Using Linked External References

Data Files

1. Open **PFSalesSum.xlsx**.
2. Save the workbook with the name **4-PFSalesSum**.
3. Open **PFQ1.xlsx**, **PFQ2.xlsx**, **PFQ3.xlsx**, and **PFQ4.xlsx**.
4. Tile all the open workbooks. *Hint: Use the Arrange All button on the View tab.*
5. Starting in cell B5 in **4-PFSalesSum.xlsx**, create formulas to populate the cells in column B by linking to the appropriate source cells in **PFQ1.xlsx**. *Hint: After creating the first formula, edit the entry in cell B5 to use a relative reference to the source cell (instead of an absolute reference) so you can copy and paste the formula in cell B5 to the range B6:B9.*
6. Create formulas to link to the appropriate source cells for the second-, third-, and fourth-quarter sales.
7. Close the four quarterly sales workbooks. Click Don't Save when prompted to save changes.
8. Maximize **4-PFSalesSum.xlsx**.
9. Make cell B5 the active cell and break the link to **PFQ1.xlsx**.
10. Print the worksheet.
11. Save and then close **4-PFSalesSum.xlsx**.

Assessment 3

Summarize Data Using 3-D References

Data Files

1. Open **JuneEntries.xlsx**.
2. Save the workbook with the name **4-JuneEntries**.
3. With AttendanceSummary the active worksheet, summarize the data in the three park worksheets using 3-D references as follows:
   a. Make cell B7 the active cell and then create a 3-D formula to sum the attendance values in the three park worksheets for day 1. Copy and paste the formula into the remaining cells in column B to complete the summary to day 16.
   b. Make cell E7 the active cell and then create a 3-D formula to sum the attendance values in the three park worksheets for day 17. Copy and paste the formula into the remaining cells in column E to complete the summary to day 30.
4. Type the label Total Vehicle and Individual Entrances in cell A24 and create a Sum formula in cell E24 to compute the grand total. Apply the Comma format with no digits after the decimal point.
5. Print the AttendanceSummary worksheet.
6. Save and then close **4-JuneEntries.xlsx**.

Assessment 4

Summarize Data in a PivotTable and PivotChart

Data Files

1. Open **BillingSummary3Q.xlsx**.
2. Save the workbook with the name **4-BillingSummary3Q**.
3. Create a PivotTable in a new worksheet as follows:
   a. Display the range named *ThirdQ* and then insert a PivotTable in a new worksheet.
   b. Add the *Attorney LName* field as rows.
   c. Add the *Area* field as columns.
   d. Sum the *Fees Due* field.
4. Apply the Pivot Style Medium 2 style (second column, first row in the *Medium* section) to the PivotTable.

5. Apply the Comma format with no digits after the decimal point to the values. Change the column widths of B through H to 13 characters. Remove the *Autofit column widths on update* check mark in the PivotTable Options dialog box. Right-align the *Martinez, O'Donovan, Sullivan, Williams,* and *Grand Total* labels in column A.
6. Name the worksheet *PivotTable* and then do the following:
   a. In cell A1, type Associate Billing Summary. Change the font to 14-point Arial and apply bold formatting. Merge and center the text across the PivotTable.
   b. In cell A2, type October - December 2018. Change the font to 14-point Arial and apply bold formatting. Merge and center the text across the PivotTable.
   c. Change the page layout to landscape orientation and then print the PivotTable.
7. Create a PivotChart from the PivotTable using the 3-D Stacked Column chart type and move the chart to its own sheet named *PivotChart.*
8. Apply Style 7 (seventh style in the Chart Styles gallery) to the PivotChart.
9. Filter the PivotChart by the attorney named *Martinez.*
10. Print the PivotChart.
11. Save and then close **4-BillingSummary3Q.xlsx.**

Assessment 5

Filter a PivotTable Using a Slicer and a Timeline

1. Open **4-BillingSummary3Q.xlsx.**
2. Save the workbook with the name **4-BillingSummary3Q-5.xlsx.**
3. Click the PivotTable sheet to view the PivotTable.
4. Remove the filter to display all the attorney names.
5. Insert a Slicer pane for the *Area* field and move the Slicer pane below the PivotTable.
6. Using the Slicer pane, filter the PivotTable by the *Corporate* field. Press and hold down the Shift key, click the button for the Divorce option, and then release the Shift key. (Hold down the Shift key to filter by multiple fields in a Slicer pane when the two fields are adjacent in the pane.)
7. Insert a Timeline pane for the *Date* field and move the Timeline pane right of the Slicer pane.
8. Using the Timeline pane, filter the PivotTable for Oct to Nov 2018.
9. Print the PivotTable.
10. Save and then close **4-BillingSummary3Q-5.xlsx.**

Assessment 6

Create and Customize Sparklines

1. Open **4-PFSalesSum.xlsx** and enable the content.
2. Save the workbook with the name **4-PFSalesSum-6.**
3. Select the range H5:H9 and insert line-type Sparklines referencing the range B5:E9.
4. Show the high point on each line using a marker.
5. Change the Sparkline color to dark blue (ninth option in the *Standard Colors* section).
6. Change the width of column H to 21 characters and type the label Region Sales by Quarter in cell H4.
7. Change the page layout to landscape orientation and then print the worksheet.
8. Save and then close **4-PFSalesSum-6.xlsx.**

Visual Benchmark

Summarize Real Estate Sales and Commission Data

1. Open **HROctSales.xlsx**.
2. Save the workbook with the name **4-HROctSales**.
3. Create the PivotTable shown in Figure WB-4.1 in a new worksheet named *PivotTable*. Apply the Pivot Style Medium 11 style and set the column widths to 18 characters. Change the page layout to landscape orientation.
4. Create the PivotChart shown in Figure WB-4.2 in a new worksheet named *PivotChart*. Use the 3-D Clustered Column chart type and apply the Style 11 style.
5. Print the PivotTable and PivotChart worksheets.
6. Save and then close **4-HROctSales.xlsx**.

Figure WB-4.1 Visual Benchmark PivotTable

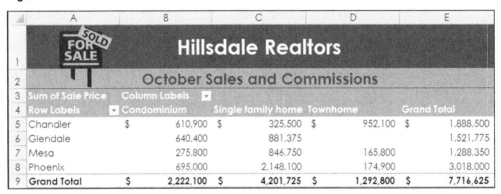

Figure WB-4.2 Visual Benchmark PivotChart

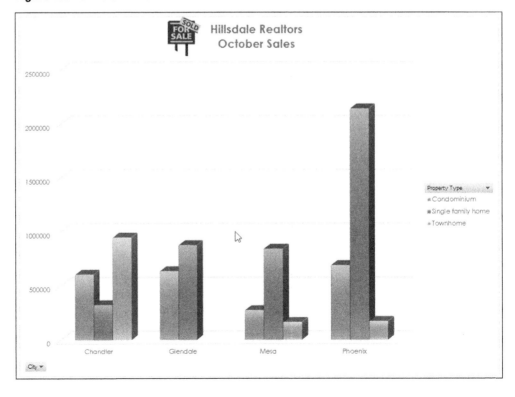

Case Study

Yolanda Robertson, your manager at NuTrends Market Research, is continuing to work on the franchise expansion plan for the owners of Pizza By Mario. Yolanda has received a new workbook from the owners with profit information by store and would like you to summarize the data. Open the workbook **PBMSales&Profits.xlsx** and review the structure of the data. Yolanda has asked you to create a PivotTable that provides the average gross sales and average net income by city and state. You determine how to organize the layout of the report. ***Hint: You can add more than one numeric field to the*** **Values** *list box*. Apply formatting options to improve the appearance of the report and make sure the report prints on one page in portrait orientation. Rename the worksheet containing the report *PivotTable*. Save the revised workbook with the name **4-PBMRpt**.

Part

2

Yolanda has asked you to create a chart that graphs the average net income data for the state of Michigan. Create a PivotChart in a new sheet named *PivotChart* and filter the chart appropriately to meet Yolanda's request. You determine the appropriate chart style and elements to include in the chart. Yolanda will use this chart at an upcoming meeting with the franchise owners and wants it to be of professional quality. Print the chart. Save the revised workbook with the name **4-PBMRpt-2** and then close the workbook.

Part

3

Open **4-PBMRpt.xlsx**. Use the Help feature to find out how to modify a numeric field setting to show values as ranked numbers, from largest to smallest. For example, instead of displaying the average value next to the city name, you will display the city's ranking as it compares with other cities in the same state. Ranking from largest to smallest means the highest value in the state is ranked as 1. Using the information you have learned in Help, change the display of the average sales to show the values ranked from largest to smallest using *City* as the base field. Remove the *Net Income* field from the PivotTable. Remove the *Grand Total* row at the bottom of the PivotTable. ***Hint: Use the Grand Totals button in the Layout group on the PivotTable Tools Design tab***. Make any other formatting changes to the report that you think will improve its appearance. Print the PivotTable. Save the revised workbook with the name **4-PBMRpt-3**.

Part

4

Yolanda has asked you to do some comparison research with another pizza franchise. Use the Internet to research the sales and net income of a pizza franchise you are familiar with. Create a new workbook that compares the total annual sales and net income values of the pizza franchise you researched with the Pizza By Mario information in **4-PBMRpt.xlsx**. Provide the URL of the website from which you obtained the information about the competitor. Create a PivotTable that presents the comparison data. Save the workbook with the name **4-PizzaFranchiseComp**. Print the comparison data. Close **4-PizzaFranchiseComp.xlsx**.

Unit 1 Performance Assessment

Assessing Proficiency

In this unit, you have learned to apply advanced formatting options, such as conditional formatting and custom number formats; perform advanced sort and filtering techniques; create functions that incorporate conditional logic, look up data, convert text, and calculate financial results; define a table and apply data management features to a table or list range; consolidate and summarize data; and present summary information in PivotTables, PivotCharts, and Sparklines.

Assessment

1

Data Files

Conditionally Format and Filter a Help Desk Worksheet

1. Open **RSRHelpDesk.xlsx**.
2. Save the workbook with the name **U1-RSRHelpDesk**.
3. Use the icon set from the Quick Analysis button to apply conditional formatting to the values in the *Priority* column.
4. Create a custom format for the values in the *Time Spent* column. The format should display a leading zero (that is, a 0 before the decimal point for a value less than 1), two digits after the decimal point, and the text *hrs* after each entry separated by one space from the number (for example, 2.20 hrs, 0.25 hrs, etc.).
5. Create two conditional formatting rules for the values in the *Time Spent* column as follows:
   a. For all the entries in which the time spent is less than one hour, apply bold formatting and the Olive Green, Accent 3, Lighter 80% fill color (seventh column, second row).
   b. For all the entries in which the time spent is more than two hours, apply the Yellow fill color (fourth column, last row).
6. Filter the worksheet by the Yellow fill color applied in the *Time Spent* column.
7. Print the filtered worksheet.
8. Clear the filter and filter arrow(s) and then print the worksheet.
9. Save and then close **U1-RSRHelpDesk.xlsx**.

Assessment 2

Use Conditional Logic Formulas in a Help Desk Worksheet

1. Open **U1-RSRHelpDesk.xlsx**.
2. Save the workbook with the name **U1-RSRHelpDesk-2**.
3. Create range names of your choosing for each of the following ranges:
   - A4:E6, which will be used in a lookup formula
   - E8:E30 in the *Operator ID* column
   - I8:I30 in the *Time Spent* column
   - J8:J30 in the *Status* column
4. In cells I5 and I6, create COUNTIF formulas to count the number of active calls (I5) and the number of closed calls (I6). Use range names in the formulas.
5. Create COUNTIF formulas in cells K3 through K6 to count the calls assigned to operator IDs 1, 2, 3, and 4, respectively. Use range names in the formulas.
6. Create SUMIF formulas in cells L3 through L6 to calculate the total time spent on calls assigned to operator IDs 1, 2, 3, and 4, respectively. Use range names in the formulas. Format the results to display two digits after the decimal point.
7. Create AVERAGEIF formulas in cells M3 through M6 to find the average time spent on calls assigned to operator IDs 1, 2, 3, and 4, respectively. Use range names in the formulas. Format the results to display two digits after the decimal point.
8. Create the HLOOKUP formula with an exact match in cell G8 to return the last name of the operator assigned to the call. Use the range name for the lookup table in the formula.
9. Create the HLOOKUP formula with an exact match in cell H8 to return the first name of the operator assigned to the call. Use the range name for the lookup table in the formula.
10. Copy the HLOOKUP formulas in the range G8:H8 and paste them into the remaining rows in the list.
11. Save, print, and then close **U1-RSRHelpDesk-2.xlsx**.

Assessment 3

Use Table and Data Management Features in a Help Desk Worksheet

1. Open **U1-RSRHelpDesk-2.xlsx**.
2. Save the workbook with the name **U1-RSRHelpDesk-3**.
3. Create the file number in column F using the ticket number in column B followed by a dash, the priority in column C followed by a dash, and the operator ID. *Hint: It may take Flash Fill a few rows before it recognizes the correct sequence.*
4. Format the range A7:J30 as a table using the Table Style Medium 20 table style.
5. Using a range name in the formula add a calculated column to the table in column K that multiplies the time spent times 15. Add the column heading *Cost* in cell K7. Apply the Comma format with two digits after the decimal point to the results.
6. Add a *Total* row to the table. Display totals for columns I and K.
7. Add emphasis to the last column in the table and band the columns instead of the rows.
8. Create a drop-down list for the *Operator ID* column that displays entries 1, 2, 3, and 4.

9. The help desk policy states that a help desk operator cannot spend more than three hours on a call. Any call that requires more than three hours must be routed to the help desk manager and assigned to another group. Create a validation rule in the *Time Spent* column that prevents any value greater than 3 from being entered. Create appropriate input and error messages. ***Note: Ignore the green triangle indicator in cell I17 that specifies that the hours should be less than or equal to 3. The green triangle indicates that the value violates the new validation rule.***

10. Type the following two records in the table above the total in row 31:

Date	3/30/2018	*Date*	3/30/2018
Ticket No.	14424	*Ticket No.*	14425
Priority	2	*Priority*	2
Type of Call	Email	*Type of Call*	Password
Operator ID	3	*Operator ID*	4
File No.	14424-2-3	*File No.*	14425-2-4
Time Spent	.75	*Time Spent*	.25
Status	Active	*Status*	Closed

11. Filter the table to display only those calls with a *Closed* status.
12. Print the filtered list.
13. Filter the worksheet to display only those calls with a *Closed* status and for which the type of call was *Password*.
14. Print the filtered list.
15. Clear both filters.
16. Save, print, and then close **U1-RSRHelpDesk-3.xlsx**.

Assessment 4 — Add Subtotals to and Outline a Help Desk Worksheet

1. Open **U1-RSRHelpDesk-3.xlsx**.
2. Save the workbook with the name **U1-RSRHelpDesk-4**.
3. Remove the *Total* row from the table.
4. Convert the table to a normal range.
5. Sort the list first by the operator's last name, then by the operator's first name, then by the call priority, and finally by the type of call—all in ascending order.
6. Add a subtotal to the list at each change in operator last name to calculate the total cost of calls by each operator.
7. Display the outlined worksheet at level 2 and then print the worksheet.
8. Display the outlined worksheet at level 3 and then print the worksheet.
9. Save and then close **U1-RSRHelpDesk-4.xlsx**.

Assessment 5 — Use Financial and Text Functions to Analyze Data for a Project

Data Files

1. Open **ACLoan.xlsx**.
2. Save the workbook with the name **U1-ACLoan**.
3. Create formulas to analyze the cost of the loan from Newfunds Trust and from Delta Capital as follows:
   a. In cells C10 and E10, calculate the monthly loan payment from each lender.
   b. In cells C12 and E12, calculate the principal portion of the first loan payment from each lender.
   c. In cells C14 and E14, calculate the total loan payment that will be made over the life of the loan from each lender.

4. In cell E20, use the text function =PROPER to return the loan company name for the loan that represents the lowest total cost to AllClaims Insurance Brokers. *Hint: The argument for the function will reference either cell C4 or cell E4*.
5. In cell E21, use the text function =LOWER to return the loan application number for the loan company name displayed in cell E20.
6. Save, print, and then close **U1-ACLoan.xlsx**.

Assessment 6

Data Files

Analyze Sales Using a PivotTable, PivotChart, and Sparklines

1. Open **PreBulkSales.xlsx**.
2. Save the workbook with the name **U1-PreBulkSales**.
3. Select the range A4:I22 and create a PivotTable in a new worksheet as follows:
   a. Add the *Category* field as the report filter field.
   b. Add the *Distributor* field as the rows.
   c. Sum the North, South, East, and West sales values.
   d. Name the worksheet *PivotTable*.
4. Apply formatting options to the PivotTable to make the data easier to read and interpret.
5. Insert a Slicer for the *Model* and show the data for *PD-1140*, *PD-1150*, and *PD-1155*.
6. Move the Slicer pane under the PivotTable and print the PivotTable and Slicer pane on one sheet.
7. Create a PivotChart and move it to a separate sheet named *PivotChart* that graphs the data from the PivotTable in a 3-D Clustered Column chart.
8. Move the legend to the bottom of the chart.
9. Apply the Style 3 format to the chart.
10. Print the chart.
11. Make Sales the active sheet and then create Sparklines in the range J5:J22 that show the North, South, East, and West sales in a line chart. Set the width of column J to 18 characters. Customize the Sparklines by changing the Sparkline color and adding data points. (You determine which data points to show and what color to make the points.) Type an appropriate label in cell J4 and add other formatting that will improve the appearance of the worksheet.
12. Save, print, and then close **U1-PreBulkSales.xlsx**.

Assessment 7

Data Files

Link to an External Data Source and Calculate Distributor Payments

1. Open **PreDistPymnt.xlsx**.
2. Save the workbook with the name **U1-PreDistPymnt**.
3. Open **U1-PreBulkSales.xlsx**.
4. Save the workbook using the name **U1-PreSource**.
5. Make the PivotTable worksheet active, remove any filters, delete the Slicer pane, and then edit the PivotTable fields so that *Sum of Total* is the only numeric field displayed in the table.
6. Save **U1-PreSource.xlsx**.
7. Arrange the display of the two workbooks vertically.
8. Create linked external references starting in cell D6 in **U1-PreDistPymnt.xlsx** to the appropriate source cells in the PivotTable in **U1-PreSource.xlsx** so that the distributor payment worksheet displays the total sales for each distributor. *Note: Since you are linking to a PivotTable, Excel automatically generates a GETPIVOTDATA function formula in each linked cell.*
9. Close **U1-PreSource.xlsx**.
10. Maximize **U1-PreDistPymnt.xlsx**.

11. Apply comma formatting with no digits after the decimal point to the range D6:D8.
12. Precision Design and Packaging pays each distributor a percentage of sales depending on the total sales achieved. The percentage for each category of sales is shown in the following chart:

Sales	Percentage
Less than $600,000	1%
Greater than or equal to $600,000 but less than $1,000,000	2%
$1,000,000 and above	4%

Calculate the payment owed for the distributors in the range H6:H8. Perform the calculation using one of the following two methods. (Choose the method that you find easiest to use.)

- Create a nested IF statement.

- Create a lookup table in the worksheet that contains the sale ranges and three percentage values. Add a column next to each distributor with a lookup formula to return the correct percentage and then calculate the payment using total sales times the percentage value.

13. Apply the Comma format with two digits after the decimal point to the range H6:H8.
14. Type TOTAL in cell B10 and then create formulas in cells D10 and H10 to calculate the total sales and total payments, respectively. Format the totals and adjust the column widths as necessary.
15. Print the worksheet. Write the GETPIVOTDATA formula for cell D6 at the bottom of the printout.
16. Break the link to the external references and convert the formulas to their existing values.
17. Save, print, and then close **U1-PreDistPymnt.xlsx**.

Writing Activities

The following activities give you the opportunity to practice your writing skills along with demonstrating an understanding of some of the important Excel features you have mastered in this unit. Use appropriate word choices and correct grammar, capitalization, and punctuation when setting up new worksheets. Also make sure that labels clearly describe the data that is presented.

Activity

1

Create a Worksheet to Track Memberships

ViewRite is offering a new membership program to its frequent customers. Customers will pay an annual membership fee that entitles them to a discount on downloads based on their membership levels. Table WB-U1.1 shows the three membership levels and discounts.

Table WB-U1.1 Activity 1

Membership Category	Annual Fee	Discount on Downloads
Gold	$45.00	15%
Silver	$30.00	12%
Classic	$20.00	10%

The manager of ViewRite has asked you to create a worksheet that will be used as a master list and includes the name of each customer participating in the membership program, the membership level the customer has paid for, and the discount the customer is entitled to receive. The worksheet should provide in list format the following information:

- Date annual membership needs to be renewed
- Customer name
- Customer telephone number
- Membership level
- Annual membership fee
- Discount level

Create a worksheet for the membership list. Use a lookup table to populate the cells containing the membership fee and discount level. Create a drop-down list for the cell containing the membership level that restricts the data entered to the three membership categories. Use a special number format for the telephone number column so that all the telephone numbers include an area code and are displayed in a consistent format. Enter a minimum of five sample records to test the worksheet with your settings.

The ViewRite manager anticipates that approximately 35 customers will subscribe to the membership program. Format enough rows with the data features to include at least 35 memberships. Save the completed worksheet with the name **U1-VRMemberships**. Print and then close the worksheet.

Activity 2

Create a Worksheet to Log Hours Walked in a Company Fitness Contest

Your company is sponsoring a contest this year to encourage employees to participate in a walking fitness program during the lunch hour. The participating employee in the department who logs the most miles or kilometers during the year will be awarded an expense-paid spa weekend at an exclusive luxury resort. You work in Human Resources and are in charge of keeping track of each department's walking record. Create a worksheet you can use to enter each department total by month and summarize the data to show the total distance walked by all participating employees at the end of the year as follows:

- Four departments have signed up for the contest: Accounting, Human Resources, Purchasing, and Marketing. Create a separate worksheet for each department.
- Each department will send you a paper copy of its employees' walking log each month. You will use this source document to enter the miles or kilometers walked by day. At the end of each month, you will calculate statistics by department to show the total distance walked, average distance walked, and number of days walked by employees during the lunch hour. When calculating the average and number of days, include only those days on which employees logged a distance. In other words, exclude from the statistics those days for which employees did not log any distance. *Hint: Consider adding a column that contains* Yes *or* No *to record whether employees participated in the walking program each day to use as the criteria range.*
- Create a summary worksheet that calculates the total miles or kilometers walked by participating employees in all four departments.

Test your settings by entering at least five days of sample data in each worksheet. Save the completed workbook with the name **U1-FitProgram**. Print the entire workbook and then close the workbook.

Optional: Using the Internet or other sources, find information on the health benefits of walking. Prepare a summary of the information and include it in a memo to employees that announces the contest. The memo is to be sent from Human Resources to all departments. Save the memo with the name **U2-FitMemo**. Print the memo and then close the file.

Internet Research

Create a Worksheet to Compare Online Auction Listing Fees

You are assisting a friend who is interested in selling a few items on an auction website on the Internet. Research a minimum of two Internet auction sites to identify all the selling and payment fees associated with selling online. For example, be sure to find out costs for the following activities involved in an auction sale:

- Listing fees (sometimes called *insertion fees*)
- Optional features that can be attached to an ad, such as reserve bid fees, picture fees, listing upgrades, and so on
- Fees paid when the item is sold based on the sale value
- Fees paid to a third party to accept a credit card payment (such as PayPal)

Create a worksheet that compares the fees for each auction website you researched. Include for each site two sample transactions and calculate the total fees that would be paid:

Sample transaction 1: Item sold for $24.99
Sample transaction 2: Item sold for $49.99

- Add optional features to the listing, such as a picture and reserve bid
- Assume in both sample transactions that the buyer pays by credit card using a third-party service

Based on your analysis, decide which auction site is the best choice from a cost perspective. Apply formatting to make the worksheet easy to read and explain your recommendation for the lower-cost auction site. Save the completed worksheet with the name **U1-AuctionAnalysis**. Print and then close the worksheet.

Microsoft®

Excel Level 2

Unit 2

Managing and Integrating Data and the Excel Environment

Microsoft® Excel®

Using Data Analysis Features

5

Study tools include a presentation and a list of chapter Quick Steps and Hint margin notes. Use these resources to help you further develop and review skills learned in this chapter.

Concepts Check

Check your understanding by identifying application tools used in this chapter. If you are a SNAP user, launch the Concepts Check from your Assignments page.

Recheck

Check your understanding by taking this quiz. If you are a SNAP user, launch the Recheck from your Assignments page.

Skills Exercise

Additional activities are available to SNAP users. If you are a SNAP user, access these activities from your Assignments page.

Skills Assessment

Assessment

1

Data Files

Convert Columns to Rows, Add Source Cells to Destination Cells, and Filter

1. Open **CRC.xlsx**.
2. Save the workbook with the name **5-CRC**.
3. Copy the range A4:F12, select cell A14, and paste the data so the columns become rows and vice versa.
4. Delete rows 4 through 13 (the original rows of source data) from the worksheet.
5. Adjust the merging and centering of the title rows across the top of the worksheet. Apply bold formatting to the range B4:I4 and AutoFit the width of each column in the worksheet.
6. Copy the values in the *Shipping* column and paste them into the *Total Cost* column using an Add operation, so that the total cost now includes the shipping fee.
7. Duplicate the validation rule for the values in the *Compact* column in the *Mid-size* and *SUV* columns. **Hint: Copy the values in the Compact *column and paste only the validation rule to the* Mid-size *and* SUV *columns.***
8. Save, print, and then close **5-CRC.xlsx**.

Assessment 2

Use Goal Seek

Data Files

1. Open **NationalBdgt.xlsx**.
2. Save the workbook with the name **5-NationalBdgt-2**.
3. Make cell D8 the active cell and open the Goal Seek dialog box.
4. Find the projected increase for wages and benefits that will make the total cost of the new budget equal $655,000.
5. Accept the solution that Goal Seek calculates.
6. Save, print, and then close **5-NationalBdgt-2.xlsx**.

Assessment 3

Use Scenario Manager

Data Files

1. Open **PreCdnTarget.xlsx**.
2. Save the workbook with the name **5-PreCdnTarget**.
3. Create scenarios to save various percentage data sets for the four regions using the following information:
   a. A scenario named *OriginalTarget* that stores the current values in the range K4:K7.
   b. A scenario named *LowSales* with the following values:
East	*0.20*
West	*0.32*
Ontario	*0.48*
Quebec	*0.37*
   c. A scenario named *HighSales* with the following values:
East	*0.36*
West	*0.58*
Ontario	*0.77*
Quebec	*0.63*
4. Show the LowSales scenario and then print the worksheet.
5. Create a scenario summary report that displays cell H18 as the result cell.
6. Print the Scenario Summary sheet.
7. Save and then close **5-PreCdnTarget.xlsx**.

Assessment 4

Create a Two-Variable Data Table

Data Files

1. Open **NationalHlpDsk.xlsx**.
2. Save the workbook with the name **5-NationalHlpDsk**.
3. Create a two-variable data table that calculates the average cost per call in the data table for each level of total call minutes logged and at each average cost per minute.
4. Save, print, and then close **5-NationalHlpDsk.xlsx**.

Assessment 5

Find and Correct Formula Errors

Data Files

1. Open **NationalCapital.xlsx**.
2. Save the workbook with the name **5-NationalCapital**.
3. Make cell D19 the active cell and use the Trace Error feature to find the source cell creating the #N/A error.
4. The manager of the Customer Service Department has reported that the cost of a Pix firewall is $4,720. Enter this data in the appropriate cell to correct the #N/A error.
5. Remove the tracer arrows.
6. The worksheet contains a logic error in one of the formulas. Find and then correct the error.
7. Save, print, and then close **5-NationalCapital.xlsx**.

Visual Benchmark

Find the Base Hourly Rate for Drum Lessons

1. Open **Lessons.xlsx**.
2. Save the workbook with the name **5-Lessons**.
3. The current worksheet is shown in Figure WB-5.1. The hourly rates in the range B5:B13 are linked to the cell named *BaseRate*, which is cell B16. For intermediate and advanced lessons, $4 and $8, respectively, is added to the hourly base rate.
4. The drum teacher wants to earn $3,531 per month from teaching lessons (instead of the current total of $3,118). Use the Goal Seek feature to change the base hourly rate to the value required to reach the drum teacher's target.
5. Save, print, and then close 5-**Lessons.xlsx**.

Figure WB-5.1 Visual Benchmark 1

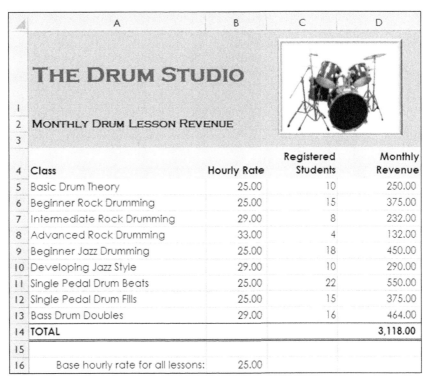

Create Scenarios for Drum Lesson Revenue

1. Open **Lessons.xlsx**.
2. Save the workbook with the name **5-Lessons-2**.
3. The drum teacher has decided to create three models for an increase in the base hourly rate charged for lessons before deciding which base rate to use next year. Examine the Scenario Summary report shown in Figure WB-5.2. Create three scenarios to save the hourly base rates shown: Low Rate Increase, Mid Rate Increase, and High Rate Increase.
4. Generate a Scenario Summary report to show the monthly revenue for each class at the three hourly base rates.

5. Format the report by changing the fill colors and font colors and adding the descriptive text in row 7. Use your best judgment in choosing colors that match those shown in Figure WB-5.2.
6. Edit the *Notes* text in cell B20 so the sentence correctly references the highlighted color for changing cells.
7. Change the page layout to landscape orientation and then print the Scenario Summary worksheet.
8. Save and then close **5-Lessons.xlsx-2**.

Figure WB-5.2 Visual Benchmark 2

			Current Values:	Low Rate Increase	Mid Rate Increase	High Rate Increase
Scenario Summary						
Changing Cells:						
	BaseRate		25.00	27.00	29.00	31.00
Result Cells:			Monthly revenue for each lesson assuming no change in number of registered students			
	BasicTheory		250.00	270.00	290.00	310.00
	BegRock		375.00	405.00	435.00	465.00
	IntRock		232.00	248.00	264.00	280.00
	AdvRock		132.00	140.00	148.00	156.00
	BegJazz		450.00	486.00	522.00	558.00
	DevJazz		290.00	310.00	330.00	350.00
	SinglePedalBeats		550.00	594.00	638.00	682.00
	SinglePedalFills		375.00	405.00	435.00	465.00
	BassDoubles		464.00	496.00	528.00	560.00
	MonthlyRevTotal		3,118.00	3,354.00	3,590.00	3,826.00

Notes: Current Values column represents values of changing cells at time Scenario Summary Report was created. Changing cells for each scenario are highlighted in green

Case Study

Part 1

Data Files

Yolanda Robertson, your manager at NuTrends Marketing Research, is continuing to work on the marketing information package for prospective new franchise owners. She has sent you a workbook named **PBMStartup.xlsx**. It contains information on the estimated capital investment required to start a new franchise, along with estimated sales and profits for the first year. The workbook calculates the number of months in which a new franchisee can expect to recoup his or her investment based on estimated sales and profits for the first year. Yolanda has asked you to use the What-If Analysis tools to find out the value required for projected sales in year 1 to pay back the initial investment in 12 months (instead of 17). Accept the proposed solution and then save the revised workbook with the name **5-PBMStartup**. Print the worksheet.

Part 2

After reviewing the printout from Part 1, Yolanda is concerned that the revised sales figure is not attainable in the first year. Before you begin modifying the file, you decide to keep a copy of the original file intact. Save the workbook with the name **5-PBMStartup-2**. Restore the sales for year 1 to the original value of $485,000. Yolanda has created the three models for the startup investment worksheet shown in Table WB-5.1. She has asked you to set up the worksheet to save all three models. *Hint: Use a comma to separate two cell references as the changing cells.* Create a report that shows the input variables for each model and how the model affects the number of months needed to recoup the initial investment. Print the summary report. Switch to the worksheet and show the model that reduces the number of months to recoup the initial investment to the lowest value. Print the worksheet. Save **5-PBMStartup-2**.

Table WB-5.1 Case Study Part 2

Conservative	Optimistic	Aggressive
$450,000	$590,000	$615,000
20%	22%	18%

Part 3

Yolanda has asked you to check the accuracy of all the formulas in the worksheet before she submits it to the client. Since you did not create this worksheet, you decide to check if there is a feature in Excel that navigates to formula cells automatically so you do not miss any calculated cells. Use the Help feature to find out how to find and select cells that contain formulas. Based on the information you learned in Help, select the cells within the worksheet that contain formulas and then review each formula cell in the Formula bar to ensure the formula is logically correct. *Hint: When the formula cells are selected as a group, press the Enter key to move to the next formula cell without losing the selection.* When you are finished reviewing the formula cells, type the name of the feature you used in a blank cell below the worksheet and then print the worksheet. Save the revised workbook with the name **5-PBMStartup-3**.

Part 4

When meeting with prospective franchise owners, Yolanda expects that individuals who do not have excellent credit ratings will find it difficult to raise the money required for the initial capital investment. Assume that the owners of Pizza by Mario are willing to finance the initial investment. Search the Internet for the current lending rate for a secured credit line at the bank at which you have an account. In a new worksheet within the workbook, document the current loan rate you found and the URL of the bank website from which you obtained the rate. Add two percentage points to the lending rate to compensate the owners for the higher risk associated with financing the startup. Rename the new worksheet as *Loan*. Create a linked cell in the Loan worksheet to the Total Estimated Initial Investment in the Startup worksheet. Calculate the monthly loan payment for a term of five years. Add appropriate labels to describe the data and format the worksheet as desired to improve its appearance. Save the revised workbook with the name **5-PBMStartup-4**. Print the loan worksheet.

Microsoft® Excel®

Protecting and Sharing Workbooks

CHAPTER 6

> **Study Tools**

Study tools include a presentation and a list of chapter Quick Steps and Hint margin notes. Use these resources to help you further develop and review skills learned in this chapter.

> **Concepts Check**

Check your understanding by identifying application tools used in this chapter. If you are a SNAP user, launch the Concepts Check from your Assignments page.

> **Recheck**

Check your understanding by taking this quiz. If you are a SNAP user, launch the Recheck from your Assignments page.

Skills Exercise

Additional activities are available to SNAP users. If you are a SNAP user, access these activities from your Assignments page.

Skills Assessment

Assessment

1

> **Data Files**

Enter and Display Workbook Properties and Insert Comments

1. Open **NationalLicenses.xlsx**.
2. Save the workbook with the name **6-NationalLicenses**.
3. Type the following text in the appropriate workbook property boxes:

Add an Author	Wendy Cheung
Title	MSO 2016 License Chargeback
Subject	Journal entry by department
Categories	JE supporting document
Status	Posted
Comments	Audit worksheet for Office 2016 site license with internal chargebacks

4. Remove the existing author, *Paradigm Publishing Inc.*
5. Make cell B8 active and insert a new comment. Type Check this quantity with Marty. The number seems high. in the comment box.
6. Make cell B14 active and insert a new comment. Type Make a note in the budget file for next year. This quantity will increase by 5. in the comment box.
7. Print the worksheet with the comments at the end of the sheet.
8. Save and then close **6-NationalLicenses.xlsx**.

Share a Worksheet, Edit a Shared Workbook, and Print a History Sheet

1. Open **PreMfgTargets.xlsx**.
2. Save the workbook with the name **6-PreMfgTargets**.
3. Share the workbook.
4. Change the user name to *Lorne Moir* and then edit the following cells:

C11	change	4,352	to	5520
C18	change	15,241	to	15960

5. Save the workbook.
6. Open a new instance of Excel. **Note: Refer to Project 2c for assistance with opening a new instance of Excel.**
7. Change the user name to *Gerri Gonzales,* open **6-PreMfgTargets.xlsx**, and then edit the following cells:

F4	change	3,845	to	5126
F9	change	7,745	to	9320

8. Save the workbook.
9. Create a history sheet to record the changes made by all the users.
10. Change the page layout to landscape orientation and then print the history sheet. **Note: If you submit your assignment work electronically, create a copy of the history sheet in a new workbook and save the workbook with the name 6-PreMfgHistory. (The history sheet is automatically deleted when the file is saved.)**
11. Save and then close both instances of **6-PreMfgTargets.xlsx**.
12. Change the user name back to the original user name for the computer you are using.

Remove Shared Access

1. Open **6-PreMfgTargets.xlsx**.
2. Save the workbook with the name **6-PreMfgTargets-3**.
3. Remove the shared access to the workbook.
4. Close **6-PreMfgTargets-3.xlsx**.

Protect an Entire Worksheet and Add a Password to a Workbook

1. Open **6-NationalLicenses.xlsx**.
2. Save the workbook with the name **6-NationalLicenses-4**.
3. Protect the entire worksheet using the password *eL2-4* to unprotect.
4. Add the password *eL2-4* to open the workbook.
5. Save and then close **6-NationalLicenses-4.xlsx**.
6. Open **6-NationalLicenses-4.xlsx** and test the password.
7. Close **6-NationalLicenses-4.xlsx**.

Unlock Cells and Protect a Worksheet and Protect a Workbook Structure

1. Open **PreMfgTargets.xlsx**.
2. Save the workbook with the name **6-PreMfgTargets-5**.
3. Select the range C4:F21 and unlock the cells.
4. Deselect the range and then protect the worksheet using the password *eL2-5* to unprotect.
5. Rename Sheet1 as *2018MfgTargets*.

6. Protect the workbook structure to prevent users from inserting, deleting, or renaming sheets using the password *eL2-5* to unprotect.
7. Save and then close **6-PreMfgTargets-5.xlsx**.

Assessment 6

Track Changes, Accept/Reject Changes, and Print a History Sheet

1. Open **6-PreMfgTargets-5.xlsx**.
2. Save the workbook with the name **6-PreMfgTargets-6**.
3. Unprotect the workbook structure so new sheets can be added, deleted, renamed, and copied.
4. Turn on the Track Changes feature.
5. Change the user name to *Grant Antone* and then edit the following cells:

   D4   change   *3,251*   to   *3755*
   D17   change   *5,748*   to   *6176*

6. Save the workbook, change the user name to *Jean Kocsis*, and then edit the following cells:

   E6   change   *6,145*   to   *5748*
   E11   change   *2,214*   to   *3417*

7. Save the workbook and then change the user name back to the original user name for the computer you are using.
8. Accept and Reject the changes in these cells as follows:

   D4   Accept
   D17   Reject
   E6   Reject
   E11   Accept

9. Create a history sheet of the changes made to the worksheet. Change the page layout to landscape orientation and then print the worksheet. ***Note: If you submit your assignment work electronically, create a copy of the history sheet in a new workbook. (The history sheet is automatically deleted when the file is saved.)***
10. Print the worksheet 2018MfgTargets.
11. Save and then close **6-PreMfgTargets-6.xlsx**.

Optional: Open **6-PreMfgTargets-6.xlsx** and email the workbook to yourself. Compose an appropriate message within the message window, as if you are an employee of Precision Design and Packaging sending the file to the office manager. Open the message window from the inbox in your email program and print the message. Close the message window and exit your email program.

Visual Benchmark

Track Changes and Insert Comments

1. Open **PawsParadise.xlsx**.
2. Save the workbook with the name **6-PawsParadise**.
3. The worksheet shown in Figure WB-6.1 includes changes made by the owner of Paradise for Paws Kennels after reviewing the worksheet created by the kennel manager. While reviewing the service price list, the owner made comments and changed cells. Using Figure WB-6.1 and Figure WB-6.2, make the same changes to your copy of the worksheet. Make sure that the changes are associated with the owner's name.

4. Create and print a history sheet scaled to fit on one page. *Note: If you submit your assignment work electronically, create a copy of the sheet in a new workbook and save the workbook with the name 6-PawsParadiseHistory. (The history sheet is automatically deleted when the file is saved.)*
5. Print the worksheet with the changes highlighted and the comments as displayed on the worksheet.
6. Save and then close **6-PawsParadise.xlsx**.
7. Change the user name back to the original user name for the computer you are using.

Figure WB-6.1 Visual Benchmark Worksheet with Comments

Figure WB-6.2 Visual Benchmark History Worksheet

Action Number	Date	Time	Who	Change	Sheet	Range	New Value	Old Value	Action Type	Losing Action
1	12/3/2018	2:50 PM	Erin Haviland	Cell Change	Prices	C4	$19.00	$18.50		
2	12/3/2018	2:50 PM	Erin Haviland	Cell Change	Prices	C7	$11.00	$10.25		
3	12/3/2018	2:50 PM	Erin Haviland	Cell Change	Prices	C10	$27.50	$25.00		
4	12/3/2018	2:50 PM	Erin Haviland	Cell Change	Prices	C14	$52.00	$48.50		
5	12/3/2018	2:51 PM	Erin Haviland	Cell Change	Prices	B7	25 minute trail walk	30 minute trail walk		

The history ends with the changes saved on 12/3/2018 at 2:51 PM.

Case Study

Yolanda Robertson, your manager at NuTrends Market Research, is working with Nicola Carlucci of Pizza by Mario on a workbook with projected franchise startups for 2018. The workbook is currently in draft format in a file named **PBMNewFranchises.xlsx**. Open the workbook and save the document as **6-PBMNewFranchises**. Add an appropriate title and subject to the workbook's properties and include a comment to explain that the draft workbook was created in consultation with Nicola Carlucci. Yolanda has asked for your assistance with protecting the workbook to prevent accidental data modifications or erasures when the workbook is shared with others. Yolanda and Nicola have agreed that the city, state, and store numbers should be protected; however, the month a new store is planned to open and the names of prospective franchisees can change. Share the workbook. Yolanda and Nicola have agreed on the following passwords:

- Password to unprotect the worksheet is *eL2-CS1*.
- Password to open the workbook is *eL2-CS1*.

Save the workbook with the name **6-PBMNewFranchises-2**. Yolanda has reviewed her research files and meeting notes and would like you to make the following changes to the data. Make sure the user name is correct so that the following changes are associated with Yolanda:

Store 138:   Franchisee is Jae-Dong Han
Store 149:   Franchisee is Leslie Posno

Save the workbook. Nicola is in charge of logistics planning and has asked you to make two changes to the months that stores are scheduled to open. Make sure the user name is correct so that the following changes are associated with Nicola:

Store 135:   Open in February
Store 141:   Open in December

Save the workbook and then display the worksheet with all the changes made by Yolanda and Nicola highlighted. Print the worksheet with the cells highlighted. Create a history sheet, change the page layout to landscape orientation, and then print it. *Note: If you submit your assignment work electronically, create a copy of the history sheet in a new workbook and save the workbook with the name* 6-PBMNewFranchisesHistory. *(The history sheet is automatically deleted when the file is saved.)* Restore the worksheet to exclusive use. Close **6-PBMNewFranchises-2.xlsx**. Change the user name back to the original user name for the computer you are using.

Yolanda is going to send the exclusive-use workbook from Part 2 to Leonard Scriver, a colleague at the Michigan office of NuTrends Market Research. Yolanda wants Leonard to review the data and add his recommendations; however, she wants him to save his copy using a different document name so that the original shared version is not changed. Open **6-PBMNewFranchises-2.xlsx**. Unprotect the worksheet, remove the password to open the workbook, and then save the workbook using the name **6-PBM-LScriver**. Based on his experience with franchise startups, Leonard makes the following recommendations, which he prefers to show in comments within the worksheet. Make sure the user name is correct so that the following comment boxes display Leonard's name:

Store 136: Opening a second store in Chicago is more likely to occur in April.

Store 144: Move this opening to June, as resources at the head office will be stretched in May.

Store 152: Try to open this franchise at the same time as store 151.

Show all the comments within the worksheet and then print it, making sure the comments print as displayed. Save and then close **6-PBM-LScriver.xlsx**. Change the user name back to the original user name for the computer that you are using.

Part 4

Mario Carlucci, owner of Pizza by Mario, has commented that the password to open the workbook is not intuitive for him and he has had trouble remembering it. He wants to change the workbook password to something more user friendly, such as *Target18*. Yolanda and Nicola chose the passwords being used in the workbook carefully based on their understanding of strong passwords that are difficult to crack by unauthorized users. Yolanda has asked you to assist in preparing a training package that will educate Mario on strong passwords. Conduct research on the Internet to find guidelines for creating strong passwords. Based on what you learn, create a document in Microsoft Word that highlights the components of a strong password. Include a table of do's and don'ts for creating strong passwords in a user-friendly, easy-to-understand format for Mario. Finally, provide a minimum of three examples that show weak passwords being improved by stronger passwords. Include a suggestion for how to use the phrasing technique to create strong passwords so they are easier to remember. Save the document with the name **6-PBMPasswords**. Print and then close **6-PBMPasswords.docx**.

Automating Repetitive Tasks and Customizing Excel

Study Tools

Study tools include a presentation and a list of chapter Quick Steps and Hint margin notes. Use these resources to help you further develop and review skills learned in this chapter.

Concepts Check

Check your understanding by identifying application tools used in this chapter. If you are a SNAP user, launch the Concepts Check from your Assignments page.

Recheck

Check your understanding by taking this quiz. If you are a SNAP user, launch the Recheck from your Assignments page.

Skills Exercise

Additional activities are available to SNAP users. If you are a SNAP user, access these activities from your Assignments page.

Skills Assessment

Create Macros

Assessment 1

1. At a new blank workbook, create the following two macros:
   a. Create a macro named *Landscape* that changes the page orientation to landscape, sets custom margins (top = 1 inch; bottom, left, and right = 0.5 inch), and centers the worksheet horizontally. Assign the macro to the keyboard shortcut key Ctrl + Shift + Q. Enter an appropriate description that includes your name and the date the macro was created.
   b. Create a macro named *Ion* that applies the Ion theme and turns off the display of gridlines in the active worksheet. Assign the macro to the keyboard shortcut Ctrl + t. Enter an appropriate description that includes your name and the date the macro was created.
2. Save the workbook as a macro-enabled workbook named **MyMacros-StudentName**, with your name substituted for *StudentName*.
3. Leave **MyMacros-StudentName.xlsm** open for the next assessment.

Run Macros

Assessment 2

Data Files

1. Open **NationalCS.xlsx**.
2. Save the workbook with the name **7-NationalCS**.
3. Press Ctrl + t to run the Ion macro.
4. Press Ctrl + Shift + Q to run the Landscape macro.
5. Save, print, and then close **7-NationalCS.xlsx**.
6. Close **MyMacros-StudentName.xlsm**.

Create Macros and Save as a Macro-Enabled Workbook

1. Open **7-NationalCS.xlsx**.
2. Create the following two macros within the current workbook:
   a. Create a macro named *FormulaBarOff* that turns off the display of the Formula bar and protects the worksheet. Do not enter a password to unprotect the sheet. Assign the macro to the keyboard shortcut Ctrl + Shift + M. Enter an appropriate description that includes your name and the date the macro was created.
   b. Create a macro named *FormulaBarOn* that turns on the display of the Formula bar and unprotects the worksheet. Assign the macro to the keyboard shortcut Ctrl + Shift + B. Enter an appropriate description that includes your name and the date the macro was created.
3. Test each macro to make sure the keyboard shortcut runs the correct commands.
4. Save the revised workbook as a macro-enabled workbook with the name **7-NationalCS-3**.
5. Close **7-NationalCS-3.xlsm**.

Print Macros

1. Open **7-NationalCS-3.xlsm** and enable the content.
2. Open the Macro dialog box and edit the FormulaBarOff macro.
3. At the Microsoft Visual Basic for Applications window with the insertion point blinking in the code window, click File on the Menu bar and then click *Print*. At the Print - VBAProject dialog box, click OK. ***Note: The FormulaBarOn macro code will also print, since both macros are stored within the VBAProject.***
4. Click File on the Menu bar and then click *Close and Return to Microsoft Excel*.
5. Close **7-NationalCS-3.xlsm**.
6. Open **MyMacros-StudentName.xlsm** and enable the content.
7. Open the Macro dialog box and edit the Landscape macro.
8. At the Microsoft Visual Basic for Applications window with the insertion point blinking in the code window, click File on the Menu bar and then click *Print*. At the Print - VBAProject dialog box, click OK. ***Note: The Ion macro code will also print, since both macros are stored within the VBAProject.***
9. Click File on the Menu bar and then click *Close and Return to Microsoft Excel*.
10. Close **MyMacros-StudentName.xlsm**.

Data Files

Customize the Excel Environment

1. Open **BillingsDec14.xlsx**.
2. Save the workbook with the name **7-BillingsDec14**.
3. Make the following changes to the display options:
   a. Turn off the horizontal scroll bar.
   b. Turn off the sheet tabs.
   c. Turn off the row and column headers.
   d. Turn off the gridlines.
4. Change the current theme to the Wisp theme.
5. Freeze the first four rows in the worksheet. Refer to Level 1 Chapter 5 for help on freezing rows.
6. Create a screen image of the worksheet with the modified display options and paste the image into a new Word document. (Use either the Print Screen and Paste or the Screen Clipping feature [Insert tab, Screenshot button, *Screen Clipping* option].) Type your name a few lines below the screen image.

7. Save the Word document with the name **7-BillingsDec14**.
8. Print **7-BillingsDec14.docx** and then exit Word.
9. Save and then close **7-BillingsDec14.xlsx**.

Assessment

6

Data Files

Create Custom Views

1. Open **BillingsDec14.xlsx**.
2. Save the workbook with the name **7-BillingsDec14-6**.
3. Select the range A4:I23 and custom sort the cells in ascending order by attorney and then by the client last name.
4. With the range A4:I23 still selected, turn on filter arrows.
5. Deselect the range and then filter the *Attorney* column to show only those rows with attorney Kyle Williams.
6. Press Ctrl + Home and create a custom view named *Williams* to save the filter settings.
7. Clear the filter in the *Attorney* column.
8. Filter the list by the attorney name *Marty O'Donovan*.
9. With cell A1 still selected, create a custom view named *O'Donovan* to save the filter settings.
10. Clear the filter in the *Attorney* column.
11. Create a custom view named *Martinez* by completing steps similar to those in Steps 8 and 9 and then clear the filter from the *Attorney* column.
12. Create a custom view named *Sullivan* by completing steps similar to those in Steps 8 and 9 and then clear the filter from the *Attorney* column.
13. Open the Custom Views dialog box. If necessary, drag the Custom Views dialog box Title bar to move the dialog box right of the worksheet. Create a screen image of the worksheet with the dialog box open and paste the image into a new Word document. (Use either the Print Screen and Paste or the Screen Clipping feature (Insert tab, Screenshot button, *Screen Clipping* option.) Type your name a few lines below the screen image.
14. Save the Word document with the name **7-BillingsDec14-6**.
15. Print **7-BillingsDec14-6.docx** and then exit Word.
16. Close the Custom Views dialog box and then save and close **7-BillingsDec14-6.xlsx**.

Assessment

7

Create and Use a Template

1. Open **7-BillingsDec14.xlsx** and turn on the display of row and column headers.
2. Make the following changes to the workbook:
   a. Select and delete all the data below the column headings in row 4.
   b. Delete the text in cell A3.
   c. Change the subtitle in cell A2 to *Associate Weekly Billing Summary*.
3. Save the revised workbook as a template named **Billings-StudentName**, with your name substituted for *StudentName*.
4. Close **Billings-StudentName.xltx**.
5. Start a new workbook based on the **Billings-StudentName.xltx** template.
6. Type December 17 to 21, 2018 in cell A3.
7. Enter the two billings shown in Table WB-7.1.
8. Save the worksheet as an Excel workbook named **7-Billings**.
9. Print and then close **7-Billings.xlsx**.
10. Copy **Billings-StudentName.xltx** from [c]\Users\username\Documents\ Custom Office Templates folder to the *EL2C7* folder on your storage medium. Close the Computer window.

Table WB-7.1   Assessment 7

File	Client	Date	Last Name	First Name	Attorney	Area	Billable Hours	Rate
IN-774	10665	12/17/2018	Rankin	Jan	Maureen Myers	Insurance	4.50	200.00
EP-895	10996	12/18/2018	Knox	Velma	Rosa Martinez	Estate	3.50	200.00

Visual Benchmark

Activity

1

Customize the Ribbon

1. Create a custom tab that includes the groups and buttons shown in Figure WB-7.1. Substitute your name for *Student Name* in the tab. All the buttons can be located using the *All Commands* list box.
2. Insert a screen image in a new Word document that shows the ribbon with the custom tab displayed in Microsoft Excel.
3. Save the Word document with the name **7-MyRibbon**.
4. Print **7-MyRibbon.docx** and then exit Word.
5. Remove the Student Name tab.

Figure WB-7.1   Visual Benchmark 1

Activity

2

Data Files

Create a Custom Template

1. Create a custom template that can be used to generate a sales invoice similar to the one shown in Figure WB-7.2. Use your best judgment to match the column widths, row heights, and color formatting. The font used in cell A1 is 36-point Footlight MT Light and the font Garamond is used for the remaining cells (18-point in cell A2 and 12-point elsewhere). Substitute an appropriate online picture if the one shown is not available on the computer you are using. The image (**VB-MusicNotes.png**) may also be accessed from the student data files. (Recall that a template should contain only text, formulas, and formatting that does not change from one workbook to another.)
2. Save the workbook as a template with the name **7-AudennitaSalesInv**.
3. Using the template, fill out a sales invoice using the data shown in Figure WB-7.2.
4. Save the completed invoice with the name **7-AudennitaInvToVanderwyst**.
5. Print the invoice and then close **7-AudennitaInvToVanderwyst.xlsx**.
6. Make a copy of the custom template and save the copy to your storage medium in the EL2C7 folder.

Figure WB-7.2 Visual Benchmark 2

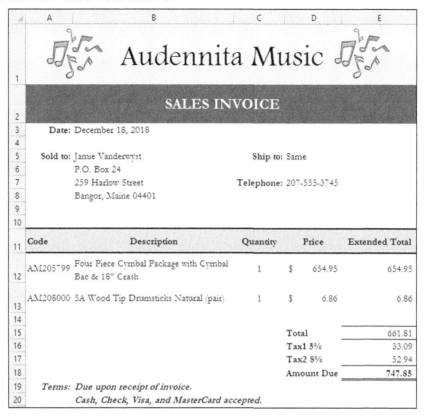

Case Study

Yolanda Robertson, your manager at NuTrends Market Research, would like you to help her become more efficient by creating macros for the frequently performed tasks in the list below. To share the macros with colleagues in the office, you decide to save all of them in a macro-enabled workbook named **7-NuTrendMacros**. Rename Sheet1 as *MacroDocumentation*. Provide documentation for each macro in the workbook by typing its name, the keyboard shortcut assigned to it, and a description of the actions it performs. This documentation will assist your colleagues in using the macros in the file. For example, in column A, type the name of the macro; in column B, type the macro's keyboard shortcut; and in column C, enter a description of the actions that the macro performs.

Create a separate macro for each of the following tasks. At the Record Macro dialog box, type your name and the current date in the *Description* text box for each macro.

- Apply the Organic theme and show all the comments.
- Set the width of the active column to 20 characters.
- Apply conditional formatting to highlight the top 10 in a selected list. Accept the default formatting options.
- Apply the Accounting format with no digits after the decimal point.
- Create a footer that prints your name centered at the bottom of the worksheet.

Print the MacroDocumentation worksheet. Open the Macro dialog box and edit the first macro. At the Microsoft Visual Basic for Applications window, print the macros in the VBAProject. Close the Visual Basic for Applications window to return to the worksheet. Save **7-NuTrendMacros.xlsm**.

Yolanda has received the file **PBMNewFranchiseRev.xlsx** from Nicola Carlucci of Pizza by Mario. She has asked you to format the workbook using the macros created in Part 1. Open the workbook and save it using the name **7-PBMNewFranchiseRev**. Run each macro created in Part 1 using the following information:

- Set the widths of all the columns to 20 characters except column C.
- Run the number formatting and conditional formatting macros with the values in column E selected.
- Run the theme and footer macros.

Print the worksheet and make sure the comments print as displayed. Save and then close **7-PBMNewFranchiseRev.xlsx**. Close **7-NuTrendsMacros.xlsm**.

Yolanda would like to customize the Quick Access Toolbar but finds it cumbersome to use the Excel Options dialog box to locate commands. Use Excel Help to learn how to add a button to the Quick Access Toolbar directly from the ribbon. Test the information you learned by adding two buttons of your choosing to the Quick Access Toolbar using the ribbon. For example, add the Orientation button from the Page Layout tab and the New Comment button from the Review tab. Using Microsoft Word, compose a memo to Yolanda that describes the steps for adding a button to the Quick Access Toolbar directly from the ribbon. Insert a screen image of the Quick Access Toolbar in Excel that displays the buttons you added below the memo text. Save the Word memo with the name **7-CustomizeQATMemo**. Print **7-CustomizeQATMemo.docx** and then exit Word. Remove the two buttons you added to the Quick Access Toolbar.

Yolanda has mentioned that she sometimes sees a *Recovered* section above the Recent list when she starts Excel. She has asked you to explain why this appears and what she should do when she sees it. Using Microsoft Word, compose a memo to Yolanda in which you explain the AutoRecover and AutoSave features in your own words. Include the explanation that the *Recovered* section appears in the opening screen after Excel has not been properly closed. Also provide advice to Yolanda on how to review the files in the Document Recovery task pane to make sure she has not lost data.

SNAP

Concepts Check

 **SNAP**

Recheck

Skills Exercise

 **SNAP**

Skills Assessment

Assessment 1

Data Files

Import Data from Access and a Text File

1. Open **HRS.xlsx**.
2. Save the workbook with the name **8-HRS**.
3. Make cell A6 active in the CPIData worksheet. Import the CPI table from the Access database **NuTrendsCensus.accdb**.
4. Make the following changes to the worksheet:
   a. Apply Table Style Medium 15 to the imported cells.
   b. Format the values in all the columns *except* column A to have one digit after the decimal point.
   c. Remove the filter arrows and then center the column headings.
   d. If necessary, adjust the column widths to accommodate the data.
5. Print the CPIData worksheet.
6. Make UIRateMI the active worksheet.
7. Make cell A6 active. Import the comma delimited text file **UIRateMI.csv**.
8. Make the following changes to the data:
   a. Change the width of the columns to 8 characters.
   b. Change the page orientation to landscape.
   c. Make any other changes that will enhance the appearance of the worksheet.
9. Print the UIRateMI worksheet.
10. Save and then close **8-HRS.xlsx**.

Assessment 2

Link Data to a Word Document

1. Open **HROctSalesByDateByRep.xlsx**.
2. Save the workbook with the name **8-HROctSalesByDateByRep-2**.
3. With SalesByDate the active worksheet, link the range A3:G27 to the end of the Word document **HROctRpt.docx**.
4. Apply narrow margins to the Word document (top, bottom, left, and right to 0.5 inch).
5. Use Save As to name the revised Word document **8-HROctRpt.docx**.
6. Switch to Excel, then press the Esc key to remove the scrolling marquee, and then deselect the range.
7. Change the value in cell F4 to *525000*.
8. Change the value in cell F5 to *212000*.
9. Save **8-HROctSalesByDateByRep-2.xlsx**.
10. Switch to Word, right-click the linked object, and then click *Update Link* at the shortcut menu.
11. Print the Word document.
12. Break the link in the Word document.
13. Save **8-HROctRpt.docx** and then exit Word.
14. Save and then close **8-HROctSalesByDateByRep-2.xlsx**.

Assessment 3

Embed Data in a PowerPoint Presentation

1. Open **HROctSalesByDateByRep.xlsx**.
2. Save the workbook with the name **8-HROctSalesByDateByRep-3**.
3. Make SalesByRep the active worksheet.
4. Display the worksheet at outline level 2 so that only the sales agent names, sale prices, and commissions display.
5. Create a column chart in a separate sheet to graph the sales commissions earned by each sales agent. You determine an appropriate chart style, title, and other chart elements.
6. Start PowerPoint and then open **HROctRpt.pptx**.
7. Save the presentation with Save As with the name **8-HROctRpt**.
8. Embed the chart created in Step 5 on Slide 3 of the presentation. Resize the chart if necessary.
9. Print the presentation as handouts with three slides displayed horizontally per page by clicking the File tab, clicking the *Print* option, clicking the *Full Page Slides* arrow, clicking the *3 Slides* option and then clicking the Print button.
10. Save **8-HROctRpt.pptx** and then exit PowerPoint.
11. Save and then close **8-HROctSalesByDateByRep-3.xlsx**.

Assessment 4

Export Data as a Text File

1. Open **HROctSalesByDateByRep.xlsx**.
2. With SalesByDate the active worksheet, save the worksheet as a CSV (comma delimited) (*.csv) text file named *8-HROctSalesByDateByRep*.
3. Close **8-HROctSalesByDateByRep.csv**. Click Don't Save when prompted to save changes.
4. Start Notepad and then open **8-HROctSalesByDateByRep.csv**.
5. Delete the first two lines at the beginning of the file, which contain the title text from the top of the worksheet. The words that should be deleted begin with the heading *Hillsdale Realtors* and end with *Commission*.
6. Delete the bottom row in the file, which contains the commas and the total commission value.

7. Print the document.

8. Save **8-HROctSalesByDateByRep.csv** and then exit Notepad.

Assessment 5

Prepare a Workbook for Distribution

1. Open **HR2018Sales.xlsx**.

2. Save the workbook with the name **8-HR2018Sales-5**.

3. Run the Accessibility Checker and correct any issues in the *Errors* section. You decide on the alternative text.

4. Display the Info backstage area and show all the properties. Read the information in the *Author, Title,* and *Subject* property text boxes. Open the Properties dialog box (by clicking *Advanced Properties* from the Properties button drop-down list) and read the information on the Statistics and Custom tabs. Close the Properties dialog box. Click the Back button and click the Review tab.

5. Turn on the display of all comments and then read the comments that appear.

6. Change to Page Layout view and check for a header or footer in the workbook.

7. Use the Document Inspector feature to check the workbook for private data and hidden information. Leave all the options selected at the Document Inspector dialog box.

8. Remove all the items that display with red exclamation marks and then close the dialog box.

9. Click the Review tab, turn off the Show All Comments feature, and switch to Normal view.

10. Click the File tab. With the Info backstage area displayed and showing all the properties, paste a screen image into a new Word document using the Print Screen with Paste or the Screenshot feature. Type your name a few lines below the screen image. Print the Word document and then exit Word without saving.

11. Run the Compatibility Checker to check for loss of functionality or fidelity in the workbook if saved in an earlier Excel version. Save the Summary report to a new sheet and then print the Compatibility Report sheet on one page.

12. Mark the workbook as final.

13. Close **8-HR2018Sales-5.xlsx**.

Assessment 6

Prepare and Distribute a Workbook

1. Open **8-HR2018Sales-5.xlsx**.

2. Save the workbook with the name **8-HR2018Sales-6**.

3. Click the Edit Anyway button.

4. Publish the workbook as a PDF file with the name **8-HR2018Sales-6**.

5. Publish the worksheet as a single file web page with the name **8-HR2018Sales-6** with the title *Hillsdale Realtors*.

6. Save and close **8-HR2018Sales-6.xlsx**.

7. Display the contents of the EL2C8 folder on your storage medium. Make sure the folder is displaying file extensions. Paste a screen image of the folder contents into a new Word document. (Use either the Print Screen and Paste or the Screen Clipping feature [Insert tab, Screenshot button, *Screen Clipping* option].) Type your name a few lines below the screen image. Print the Word document and then exit Word without saving. Close the Computer or Documents window.

Visual Benchmark

Import, Analyze, and Export Population Data

1. Look at the data in the worksheet shown in Figure WB-8.1. Create this worksheet by importing the PopByState table from the Access database **NuTrendsCensus.accdb** into a new worksheet. Once imported, the rows and columns included in the database table but not shown in the figure were deleted and the filter arrows removed. In addition, the Table Style Light 2 style has been applied to the worksheet. Add the title rows at the top of the imported data and change the title in cell B4 as shown. Use your best judgment to match other formatting characteristics, such as column width, row height, number formatting, alignment, and fill color.

2. Rename the worksheet with the name *PopulationTable* and then print it.

3. Select the range A4:B18 and create the chart shown in Figure WB-8.2 in a new worksheet with the name *PopulationChart*. The chart has the Style 3 style applied. The *Rounded Rectangle* in the Insert Shapes group on the Chart Tools Format tab was used to insert the source information. Use the Shape Effects button in the Shape Styles group to apply the shadow. Use your best judgment to match the other chart options and formatting with those shown in the chart.

4. Save the workbook with the name **8-PBMPopData**.

5. Start Microsoft Word and then open **PBMReport.docx**. Rename the workbook **8-PBMReport**. Change *Student Name* on page 1 to your name. Copy and paste the Excel chart, positioning the chart between the last two paragraphs on page 2 of the document. Make any formatting adjustments to the chart that are necessary once the chart has been inserted. Save, print, and then close **8-PBMReport.docx**.

6. Close **8-PBMPopData.xlsx**.

Figure WB-8.1 Visual Benchmark PopulationTable Worksheet

	A	B
1	**U.S. Population Estimates as of July 1, 2014**	
2	**US Census Bureau**	
3	**States Selected for Franchise Expansion**	
4	State	Population
5	Illinois	12,880,580
6	Indiana	6,596,855
7	Kansas	2,904,021
8	Kentucky	4,413,457
9	Michigan	9,909,877
10	Minnesota	5,457,173
11	Missouri	6,063,589
12	Montana	1,023,579
13	Nebraska	1,881,503
14	North Dakota	739,482
15	Ohio	11,594,163
16	South Dakota	853,175
17	Wisconsin	5,757,564
18	Wyoming	584,153

Figure WB-8.2 Visual Benchmark PopulationChart Chart

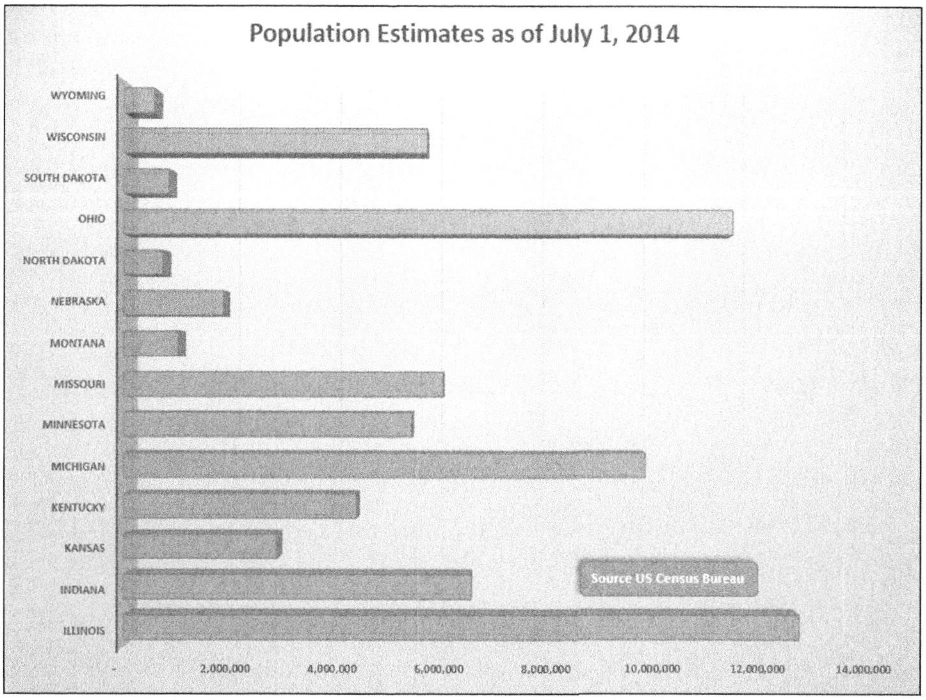

Case Study

Yolanda Robertson, your manager at NuTrends Market Research, has asked you to provide new research data from the US Census Bureau for her Pizza by Mario franchise expansion project. The franchise expansion is planned for the states of Illinois, Indiana, and Kentucky. Start a new workbook and set up three worksheets named with the state names. In each sheet, import the People Quickfacts table for the state using the **IlinoisQF.txt**, **IndianaQF.txt**, and **KentuckyQF.txt** data files. Once the data is imported in each worksheet, add an appropriate title, merged and centered above the imported data, and apply formatting enhancements to improve the appearance of the column headings. Save the workbook with the name **8-PBMResearch**. Print all three worksheets.

To prepare for an upcoming meeting with Mario and Nicola Carlucci of Pizza by Mario, Yolanda has asked you to copy selected information from each state to a Word document. Open **PBMExpansionResearch.docx**. Save the document with the name **8-PBMExpansionResearch**. From the Excel workbook you created in Part 1, copy and paste into the Word document the following data for each state. (Do not include the data in the *USA* column.) Do not embed or link the data because the information will not be changed or updated.

> Households
> Persons per household
> Median household income

If the data you imported does not contain these headings, locate and copy information closely related to number of households and income for each state.

Save, print, and then close **8-PBMExpansionResearch.docx**. Close **8-PBMResearch.xlsx**.

Part 3

Yolanda has asked you to save the workbook as a web page (*.htm,*.html). Research in Excel Help the different options in the Browser View Options dialog box. Also, search the Internet for at least two web-hosting providers. Using Microsoft Word, compose a memo to Yolanda that briefly explains the options in the Browser View Options dialog box in Excel. (Be sure to compose the explanation using your own words.) Include in the memo the URLs of the two web-hosting providers you visited and add your recommendation for the provider you want to use. Save the memo with the name **8-WebMemo**. Print and then close **8-WebMemo.docx** and then exit Word.

Microsoft

Excel Level 2

Unit 2 Performance Assessment

Assessing Proficiency

In this unit, you learned to use features in Excel that facilitate performing "What if?" analyses, identifying relationships between worksheet formulas, collaborating with others by sharing and protecting workbooks, and automating repetitive tasks using macros. You also learned how to customize the Excel environment to suit your preferences and to integrate Excel data by importing it from and exporting it to external sources. Finally, you learned how to prepare and distribute a workbook to others by removing items that are private or confidential, marking the workbook as final, checking for features incompatible with earlier versions of Excel, and saving and sending a worksheet in various formats.

Assessment

1

Data Files

Use Goal Seek and Scenario Manager to Calculate Investment Proposals

1. Open **HillsInvtPlan.xlsx**.
2. Save the workbook with the name **U2-HillsInvtPlan**.
3. Use Goal Seek to find the monthly amount the client must contribute to increase the projected value of the plan to $65,000 at the end of the term. Accept the solution that Goal Seek calculates.
4. Assign the range name *AvgReturn* to cell E8.
5. Create three scenarios for changing cell E8 as follows:

Scenario name	Return rate
Moderate	5.5%
Conservative	4.0%
Aggressive	12.5%

6. Apply the Aggressive scenario and then print the worksheet.
7. Change the Moderate scenario's investment return rate to 8.0% and then apply the scenario.
8. Create and then print a scenario summary report.
9. Save and then close **U2-HillsInvtPlan.xlsx**.

Assessment

2

Data Files

Calculate Investment Outcomes for a Portfolio Using a Two-Variable Data Table

1. Open **HillsResearchInvtTbl.xlsx**.
2. Save the workbook with the name **U2-HillsResearchInvtTbl**.
3. Create a two-variable data table that calculates the projected value of the investment plan at the end of the term for each monthly contribution payment and at each interest rate in the range A11:G20.
4. Apply the Comma format to the projected values in the table and adjust the column widths as necessary.
5. Make cell E8 active and display precedent arrows.
6. Make cell A11 active and display precedent arrows.
7. Remove the arrows.
8. Save, print, and then close **U2-HillsResearchInvtTbl.xlsx**.

Assessment

3

Data Files

Solve an Error and Check for Accuracy in Investment Commission Formulas

1. Open **HillsModPortfolio.xlsx**.
2. Save the workbook with the name **U2-HillsModPortfolio**.
3. Solve the #VALUE! error in cell E19. Use formula auditing tools to help find the source cell that contains the invalid entry.
4. Check the logical accuracy of the formula in cell E19 by creating proof formulas below the worksheet as follows:
   a. In row 21, calculate the amount from the customer's deposit that is deposited into each of the six funds based on the percentages in column B. For example, in cell B21, create a formula to multiply the customer's deposit in cell B19 ($5,000.00) by the percentage recommended for investment in the DW Bond fund in cell B5 (40%). Create similar formulas for the remaining funds in the range C21:G21.
   b. In row 22, multiply the amount deposited to each fund by the fund's commission rate. For example, in cell B22, create a formula to multiply the value in cell B21 ($2,000.00) by the commission rate paid by the DW Bond fund in cell B17 (1.15%). Create similar formulas for the remaining funds in the range C22:G22.
   c. In cell B23, use the SUM function to calculate the total of the commissions for the six funds in the range B22:G22.
   d. Add appropriate labels next to the values created in rows 21 through 23.
5. Save, print, and then close **U2-HillsModPortfolio.xlsx**.

Assessment

4

Document and Share a Workbook and Manage Changes in an Investment Portfolio Worksheet

1. Open **U2-HillsModPortfolio.xlsx**.
2. Save the workbook with the name **U2-HillsModPortfolio-4**.
3. Type the following data into the workbook properties. *Note: If any of the properties currently contains text, replace it with the entry below.*

Author	Logan Whitmore
Title	Recommended Moderate Portfolio
Comments	Proposed moderate fund
Subject	Moderate Investment Allocation

4. In a new Word document, paste a screenshot of the Info backstage area with all the properties visible. Type your name a few lines below the image, print the document, and then close Word without saving.
5. Click the Review tab and then share the workbook.

6. Change the user name to *Carey Winters* and then edit the cells as follows:

    B7   change *10%* to *15%*
    B8   change *15%* to *10%*

7. Save **U2-HillsModPortfolio-4.xlsx**.
8. Change the user name to *Jodi VanKemenade* and then edit the cells as follows:

    D17 change *2.15%* to *2.32%*
    E17 change *2.35%* to *2.19%*

9. Save **U2-HillsModPortfolio-4.xlsx**.
10. Create and then print a History worksheet on one page. *Note: If you are to submit your assignment electronically, create a copy of the History worksheet in a new workbook named U2-HillsModPortfolioHistory.*
11. Change the user name back to the original name on the computer you are using.
12. Accept and reject the changes made to the cells in the ModeratePortfolio worksheet as follows:

    B7   Reject
    B8   Reject
    D17   Accept
    E17   Reject

13. Save, print, and then close **U2-HillsModPortfolio-4.xlsx**.

Assessment 5

Insert Comments and Protect a Confidential Investment Portfolio Workbook

1. Open **U2-HillsModPortfolio-4.xlsx**.
2. Save the workbook with the name **U2-HillsModPortfolio-5**.
3. Remove the shared access to the workbook.
4. Hide rows 20 through 23.
5. Make cell B17 the active cell and insert a comment. Type Commission rate to be renegotiated in 2018 in the comment box.
6. Copy the comment in cell B17 and paste it into cells D17 and G17. Press the Esc key to remove the scrolling marquee from cell B17.
7. Edit the comment in cell G17 to change the year from *2018* to *2019*.
8. Protect the worksheet to allow editing only in cell B19. Assign the password *eL2-U2* to unprotect the worksheet.
9. Encrypt the workbook with the password *eL2-U2*.
10. Save and close **U2-HillsModPortfolio-5.xlsx**.
11. Test the security features added to the workbook by opening **U2-HillsModPortfolio-5.xlsx** using the password created in Step 9. Try to change one of the values in the range B5:B10 and in the range B17:G17.
12. Make cell B19 active and then change the value to *10000*.
13. Display all the comments in the worksheet and then print the worksheet with the comments displayed and with the worksheet scaled to fit on one page.
14. Save and then close **U2-HillsModPortfolio-5.xlsx**.

Assessment

6

Automate and Customize an Investment Portfolio Workbook

1. Open **U2-HillsModPortfolio-5.xlsx**.
2. Unprotect the worksheet, turn off the display of all comments, and then delete the comments in cells B17, D17, and G17.
3. Display the Custom Views dialog box. When a workbook is shared, Excel automatically creates a custom view (with the label *Personal View*) for each person who accesses the file and for the original worksheet state before sharing was enabled. Delete all the custom views in the dialog box and then add a new custom view named *ModeratePortfolioOriginalView*.
4. Create two macros to be stored in the active workbook as follows:
   a. Create a macro named *CustomDisplay* that applies the Metropolitan theme and turns off the display of gridlines and row and column headers in the current worksheet. Assign the macro to the keyboard shortcut Ctrl + Shift + T. Enter an appropriate description that includes your name and the date the macro was created.
   b. Create a macro named *CustomHeader* that prints the text *Private and Confidential* at the left margin in the header. Assign the macro to the keyboard shortcut Ctrl + Shift + H. Enter an appropriate description that includes your name and the date the macro was created.
5. Test the macros by opening **U2-HillsInvtPlan.xlsx**. Make InvestmentPlanProposal the active worksheet and then run the two macros created in Step 4. View the worksheet in the Print backstage area. Close the Print backstage area and then close **U2-HillsInvtPlan.xlsx** without saving the changes.
6. Print the VBA program code for the two macros and then close the Microsoft Visual Basic for Applications window and return to Excel.
7. Create a custom view named *ModeratePortfolioTemplateView*.
8. Remove the password to open the workbook and then save the revised workbook as a macro-enabled workbook with the name **U2-HillsModPortfolio-6**.
9. Print the worksheet.
10. Display the Custom Views dialog box. Paste a screenshot of the worksheet with the Custom Views dialog box open into a new Word document. Type your name a few lines below the image, print the document, and then exit Word without saving.
11. Close the Custom Views dialog box and save and then close **U2-HillsModPortfolio.xlsm**.

Assessment

7

Create and Use an Investment Planner Template

1. Open **U2-HillsResearchInvtTbl.xlsx**.
2. Make the following changes to the worksheet:
   a. Change the label in cell A3 to *Investment Planner*.
   b. Change the font color of cell A11 to White. This will make the cell appear to be empty. (You want to disguise the entry in this cell because displaying the value at the top left of the data table may confuse Hillsdale customers.)
   c. Clear the contents of the range E5:E7.
   d. Protect the worksheet so that editing is allowed only in the range E5:E7. Assign the password *eL2-U2* to unprotect the worksheet.
3. Save the revised workbook as a template with the name **HillsInvPlan-StudentName**, substituting your name for *StudentName*.

4. Close **HillsInvPlan-StudentName.xltx**.
5. Start a new workbook based on the **HillsInvPlan-StudentName.xltx** template.
6. Type the following information in the appropriate cells:

Monthly contribution:	-475
Number of years to invest:	5
Forecasted annual interest rate:	4.75%

7. Save the workbook as an Excel workbook with the name **U2-HillsInvPlan-7**.
8. Print and then close **U2-HillsInvPlan-7.xlsx**.
9. Copy the template created in this assessment to the EL2U2 folder on your storage medium.

Assessment

8

Export a Chart and Prepare and Distribute an Investment Portfolio Worksheet

1. Open **U2-HillsModPortfolio-6.xlsm**. If a security warning appears, enable the content.
2. Start Microsoft PowerPoint 2016 and then open **HillsPortfolios.pptx**.
3. Save the presentation with the name **U2-HillsPortfolios**.
4. Copy the pie chart from the Excel worksheet to Slide 7 in the PowerPoint presentation.
5. Resize the chart on the slide and edit the legend if necessary to make the chart consistent with the other charts in the presentation.
6. Print the PowerPoint presentation as a handout with nine slides printed horizontally on the page.
7. Save **U2-HillsPortfolios.pptx** and then exit PowerPoint.
8. Deselect the chart in the Excel worksheet.
9. Inspect the document, leaving all items checked at the Document Inspector dialog box.
10. Remove all the items that display with red exclamation marks and Remove All buttons. Close the dialog box.
11. Change the file type to a workbook with an *.xlsx* file extension with the name **U2-HillsModPortfolio-8**. Click Yes at the message stating that the file cannot be saved with the VB Project. Click OK at the privacy warning message box.
12. Mark the workbook as final. Click OK if the privacy warning message box reappears.
13. Send the workbook to yourself as an XPS document in an email initiated from Excel. Include an appropriate message in the message window, assuming that you work for Hillsdale Financial Services and are sending the portfolio file to a potential client. Open the message window from the inbox in your email program and then print it. Close the message window and exit the email program.
14. Display the Info backstage area and make sure all the properties are visible. Take a screenshot and paste it into a new Word document. Type your name a few lines below the image, print the document, and then exit Word without saving.
15. Save and close **U2-HillsModPortfolio-8.xlsx**.

Writing Activities

The following activities give you the opportunity to practice your writing skills while demonstrating an understanding of some of the important Excel features you have mastered in this unit. Use appropriate word choices and correct grammar, capitalization, and punctuation when setting up new worksheets. Labels should clearly describe the data that is presented.

Create a Computer Maintenance Template

The Computing Services Department of National Online Marketing Inc. wants to create a computer maintenance template that help desk employees will complete electronically and save to a document management server. This system will make it easy for a technician to check the status of any employee's computer from any location within the company. Help Desk employees perform the following maintenance tasks at each computer twice annually:

- Delete temporary Internet files
- Delete temporary document files that begin with a tilde (~)
- Update hardware drivers
- Reconfirm all serial numbers and asset records
- Have the employee change his or her password
- Check that automatic updates for the operating system are active
- Check that automatic updates for virus protection are active
- Confirm that automatic backup to the computing services server is active
- Confirm that the employee is archiving all email messages
- Clean the computer's screen, keyboard, and system unit

In a new workbook, create a template that can be used to complete the maintenance form electronically. The template should include information that identifies the workstation by the asset ID number, the department in which the computer is located, the name of the employee that uses the computer, the name of the technician that performs the maintenance, and the date the maintenance is performed. In addition, include a column that provides a drop-down list with these options next to each task: *Completed*, *Not Completed*, and *Not Applicable*. Next to this column, include a column in which the technician can type notes. At the bottom of the template, include a text box and type the following message in it:

> Save using the file naming standard CM-StationID##-yourinitials, where ## is the asset ID. Example: CM-StationID56-JW

Protect the worksheet, leaving unlocked the cells that the technician will fill in as he or she completes a maintenance visit. Do not include a password for unprotecting the sheet. Save the template with the name **NationalCMForm-StudentName**, substituting your name for *StudentName*. Start a new workbook based on the custom template. To test the organization and layout of the template, fill out a form as if you are a technician working on your own computer. Save the completed form as an Excel workbook with the name **U2-Act1-NationalCMForm**. Print the form scaled to fit on one page. Copy **NationalCMForm-StudentName.xltx** to your storage medium.

Internet Research

Apply a "What If?" Analysis to a Planned Move

Following graduation, you plan to move out of the state/province for a few years to live on your own. Create a new workbook to use as you plan this move to develop a budget for expenses in the first year. Research typical rents for apartments in the city in which you want to find your first job. Estimate other living costs in the city, including transportation, food, entertainment, clothes, telephone, cable/satellite, cell phone, Internet, and so on. Calculate total living costs for an entire year.

Also, research annual starting salaries for your chosen field of study in the same area. Estimate the take-home pay at approximately 70% of the annual salary you decide to use. Using the take-home pay and the total living costs for the year, calculate whether you will have enough money to cover your expenses.

Assume that you want to save money to go on a vacation at the end of the year. Use Goal Seek to find the take-home pay you need to earn to have $2,000 left over at the end of the year. Accept the solution that Goal Seek provides and then create two scenarios in the worksheet as follows:

- A scenario named LowestValues, in which you adjust each value down to the lowest amount you think is reasonable
- A scenario named HighestValues, in which you adjust each value up to the highest amount you think is reasonable

Apply each scenario and notice the effect on the amount left over at the end of the year. Display the worksheet in the HighestValues scenario and then create a scenario summary report. Print the worksheet, applying print options as necessary to minimize the pages required. Print the scenario summary report. Save the workbook as **U2-MyFirstYearBudget** and then close the file.

Research and Compare Smartphones

You work for an independent marketing consultant who travels frequently in North America and Europe for work. The consultant, Lindsay Somers, would like to purchase a smartphone. While traveling, she will use the smartphone for conference calls, email, web browsing, text messaging, and modifying PowerPoint presentations, Word documents, and Excel worksheets. Using the Internet, research the latest smartphones from three different manufacturers. Prepare a worksheet that compares the three smartphones, organizing the information so the main features are shown along the left side of the page by category and the different phones' specifications for these features are set in columns. At the bottom of each column, provide the hyperlink to the phone's specifications on the web.

Based on your perception of the best value, select one of the phones and use a comment box in the worksheet to recommend the phone to Lindsay. In the comment box, provide a brief explanation of why you chose this phone. Make sure all the comments display in the worksheet. Save the worksheet with the name **U2-Smartphones**. Publish the worksheet as a single file web page, accepting the default file name and changing the page title to *Smartphone Feature and Price Comparison*. Print the web page from the Microsoft Edge window. Close Microsoft Edge and then close **U2-Smartphones.xlsx**.

Job Study

Prepare a Wages Budget and Link the Budget to a Word Document

You work at a small, independent, long-term care facility named Gardenview Place Long-Term Care. As the assistant to the business manager, you are helping to prepare next year's hourly wages budget. Create a worksheet to estimate next year's hourly wage expenses using the average wage costs in Table WB-U2.1 and the following information about hourly paid workers:

- The facility runs three 8-hour shifts, 7 days per week, 52 weeks per year: 6 a.m. to 2 p.m., 2 p.m. to 10 p.m., and 10 p.m. to 6 a.m.
- Each shift requires two registered nurses, four licensed practical nurses, and two healthcare aid workers.
- On each shift, one of the registered nurses is designated as the charge nurse and is paid a premium of 15% his or her regular hourly rate.
- The shifts from 6 a.m. to 2 p.m. and 2 p.m. to 10 p.m. require one custodian; the shift from 10 p.m. to 6 a.m. requires two custodians.
- Each shift requires the services of an on-call physician and on-call pharmacist. Budget for the physician and pharmacist at 4 hours per shift.
- Add 14% to the total wage costs for each shift to cover the estimated costs of benefits such as vacation pay, holiday pay, and medical care coverage for all workers *except* the on-call physician and on-call pharmacist as they do not receive these benefits.

Make use of colors, themes, and table features to make the budget calculations workbook easy to read. Save the workbook with the name **U2-GardenviewWageBdgt**. Print the worksheet, adjusting print options as necessary to minimize the pages required. Create a chart in a separate sheet to show the total hourly wages budget by worker category. You determine the chart type and chart options to use in presenting the information.

Start Word and open **GardenviewOpBdgt.docx**. Change the year on the title page of the document to the current year. Change the name and date at the bottom of the title page to your name and the current date. Link the chart created in the Excel worksheet to the end of the Word document. Save the revised document with the name **U2-GardenviewOpBdgt**. Print and then close **U2-GardenviewOpBdgt.docx**. Deselect the chart and close it.

Table WB-U2.1 Average Hourly Wage Rates

Wage Category	Average Wage Rate
Registered nurse	$32.64
Licensed practical nurse	$19.63
Healthcare aid worker	$16.05
Custodian	$15.96
On-call physician	$75.00
On-call pharmacist	$52.00